WAR IN THE HORN
The Conflict between Eritrea and Ethiopia

Patrick Gilkes and Martin Plaut

THE ROYAL INSTITUTE OF
INTERNATIONAL AFFAIRS

Published in Great Britain in 1999 by the Royal Institute of International Affairs,
Chatham House, 10 St James's Square, London SW1Y 4LE (Charity Registration No. 208 223)

ISBN 1 86203 059 6

Printed and bound in Great Britain by the Chameleon Press Limited

The Royal Institute of International Affairs publishes RIIA Discussion Papers to make research results, policy discussions and important background information available as speedily as possible and in a concise manner to those concerned with international policy issues. The series thus provides summaries of work that may subsequently be published in a more substantial form.

The Royal Institute of International Affairs, at Chatham House in London, has provided an independent forum for discussion and debate on current international issues for nearly 80 years. Its resident research fellows, specialized information resources, and range of publications, conferences and meetings span the fields of international politics, economics and security. The Institute does not express opinions of its own; the views expressed in this publication are the responsibility of the authors.

CONTENTS

ABOUT THE AUTHORS

Patrick Gilkes is a consultant on the Horn of Africa, and was formerly Head of the BBC Somali service.

Martin Plaut is an Associate Fellow of the Royal Institute of International Affairs and is Output Editor for the BBC World Service.

ACKNOWLEDGMENTS

The authors would like to acknowledge the assistance they received from many participants in the current conflict, as well as a number of observers of the Horn, none of whom wished to be named. We also wish to thank George Joffé, the Director of Studies at Chatham House, for his support and encouragement for this study, and Margaret May, Head of Publications, for her untiring efforts in bringing the document to publication.

The paper takes the conflict to the end of August 1999, since when there has been a further US mission to Ethiopia, led by Susan Rice, and a report of another outbreak of fighting along the border. But by the time of going to press, early in September, there was no sign of a resolution of the dispute.

September 1999   P.G.
                                                                                                        M.P.

SUMMARY

The war that broke out between Ethiopia and Eritrea in May 1998 is one of the bloodiest of recent times. Yet prior to the fighting these neighbours were governed by movements that were close allies, and led by men who had been personal friends.

This discussion paper examines the region's pre-colonial past and the impact of the settlement after the Second World War. It suggests how differing concepts of nationalism developed for the TPLF and the EPLF, the two liberation movements that overthrew the Ethiopian regime in 1991, and charts the chequered record of cooperation between them.

The paper outlines the unfolding of the dispute, from a small-scale skirmish on an ill-defined border to a heavy military confrontation including the use of tanks, air power and massive numbers of ground troops. It describes the spread of the conflict, its economic and human consequences and the diplomatic efforts within the region, on the continent and by the international community. The study contains several of the key documents laying out the diplomatic initiatives by the United States, Rwanda and the Organization of African Unity to resolve the crisis.

The authors conclude with a number of specific questions that the conflict raises for the region and the prospects for peace. They ask whether there is a satisfactory solution to the present stalemate, in the face of intransigence by both sides, despite the tantalizingly small gap between the two parties.

Map 1: The Horn of Africa

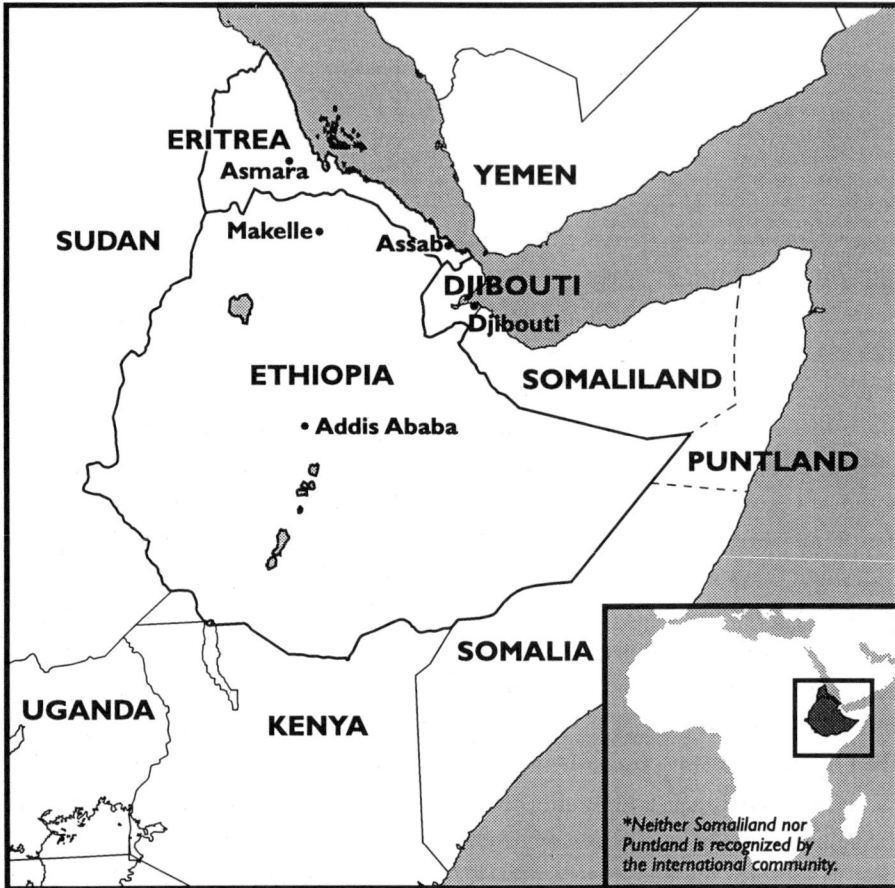

ERITREA
Asmara
YEMEN
SUDAN
Makelle•
•Assab
DJIBOUTI
•Djibouti
ETHIOPIA
SOMALILAND
• Addis Ababa
PUNTLAND
SOMALIA
UGANDA
KENYA

*Neither Somaliland nor Puntland is recognized by the international community.

Map 2: The contested border

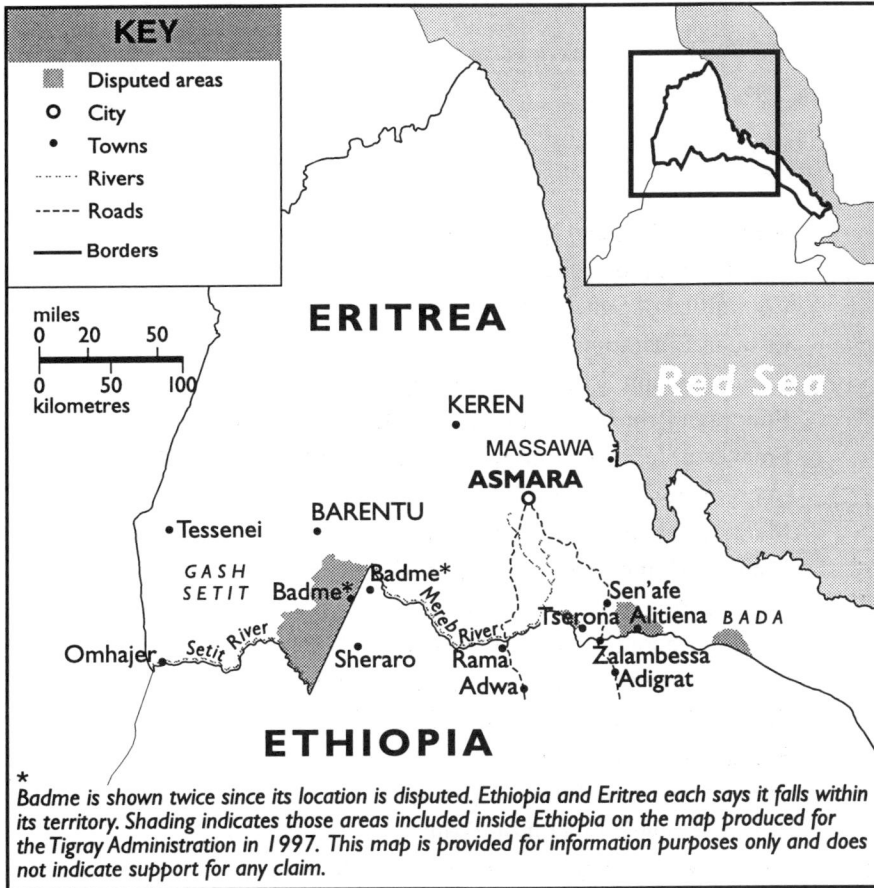

KEY

- Disputed areas
- ○ City
- • Towns
- ⋯⋯ Rivers
- ----- Roads
- ——— Borders

miles
0 20 50

0 50 100
kilometres

ERITREA

Red Sea

KEREN
•

MASSAWA
•

ASMARA
○

• Tessenei

BARENTU
•

GASH
SETIT

Badme* • Badme*

Sen'afe •
Tserona Alitiena BADA
•   •

Omhajer • Setit River

Sheraro •
Rama •
Adwa •

Zalambessa •
Adigrat •

ETHIOPIA

*
Badme is shown twice since its location is disputed. Ethiopia and Eritrea each says it falls within its territory. Shading indicates those areas included inside Ethiopia on the map produced for the Tigray Administration in 1997. This map is provided for information purposes only and does not indicate support for any claim.

ABBREVIATIONS

AENF	Alliance of Eritrean National Forces
ALF	Afar Liberation Front
Comessa	Committee of Sahel-Saharan States
ELF	Eritrean Liberation Front
EPLF	Eritrean People's Liberation Front
EPRDF	Ethiopian People's Revolutionary Democratic Front
FRUD	Front pour la Restauration de l'Unité et la Démocratie (Djibouti)
IGAD	Intergovernmental Agency for Development
MLLT	Marxist Leninist League of Tigray
NDA	National Democratic Alliance (Sudan)
OAU	Organization of African Unity
OLF	Oromo Liberation Front (Ethiopia)
ONLF	Oromo National Liberation Front (Ethiopia)
PFDJ	Popular Front for Democracy and Justice
SNF	Somali National Front
TLF	Tigray Liberation Front
TPLF	Tigray People's Liberation Front
UNHCR	United Nations High Commission for Refugees

1 INTRODUCTION

In May 1991 the capital of Eritrea, Asmara, fell to the liberation movement that had been fighting for the independence of the territory for the last thirty years. At the same time the Ethiopian capital, Addis Ababa, was captured by forces led by northern rebels from the province of Tigray. It seemed, for a moment, that the long and bloody wars that had racked the region might be at an end. The dual victories were the result of a close cooperation between the two movements that had led these struggles – the Eritrean People's Liberation Front (EPLF) and the Tigray People's Liberation Front (TPLF). Both had been determined to overcome authoritarian rule from Addis Ababa and had worked closely together to achieve this end. Two years later Eritrea achieved formal independence, recognized by the United Nations, by the Organization of African Unity (OAU) and – most important of all – by the new rulers in Ethiopia.

At the hour of victory relations between the two movements appeared warm and friendly. Yet just seven years later the divisions could hardly be deeper. Since May 1998 they have been at war. Their leaders, who were once close personal friends, are no longer on speaking terms. Tens of thousands of people have been deported or felt compelled to return to their respective homelands and their radio stations blare out vitriolic propaganda against each other.

The circumstances of this remarkable turn of events are already complex and, further, have been obscured by the contradictory versions of the truth that both sides have advanced. The authors of this brief study have done their best to disentangle fact from fiction, and much of what follows is the result of discussions, on and off the record, with participants in the events either in the region or abroad. Aspects of what took place are still far from clear and the account provided here is certain to be contested by each of the parties to the conflict.

2 A TROUBLED HISTORY

Until the end of the nineteenth century Ethiopia was rarely more than a loose confederation of kingdoms. The empire was alternatively dominated by Amhara or Oromo princes from the provinces of Gondar and Wollo in the centre of the country, or by Tigray rulers from the northern region of Tigray, which included the Tigrinya-speaking areas of what is now Eritrea. The boundaries of the empire were fluid. When Tigray princes were in the ascendancy they extended their influence towards the Red Sea coast of Eritrea, exacting tribute from the Muslim lowland chiefs around Massawa or in the west. They brought Coptic Christianity to the highlands of Eritrea, while the lowlands along the coast and towards the western border with Sudan remained Muslim.

In the sixteenth century the coastal plain of Eritrea became part of the Ottoman empire, though for most of the seventeenth and eighteenth centuries the rulers of the coast, who were appointed by the Ottoman Pasha of Jeddah, also acknowledged the overlordship of the rulers of Tigray. As the Ottoman empire declined, Egypt inherited its place along the Red Sea coasts, first taking over Massawa in the 1820s. In the 1870s, the Tigray Emperor Yohannis IV (1872–89) defeated two Egyptian attempts to penetrate the highlands of Eritrea. Subsequently he believed that in return for allowing the evacuation of Egyptian garrisons from Sudan after the rise of the Mahdi, he had British and Egyptian agreement to take over Massawa. In the event, Britain, worried about expanding French influence in Africa, encouraged Italy (which had laid claim to Assab in 1870) to take Massawa in 1885. Yohannis, rightly, felt betrayed, the more so as Italy promptly attempted to use Massawa as a base from which to extend its influence into Ethiopia. But the Italians' hopes were dashed when they were defeated in 1896 by the Ethiopian forces of Emperor Menelik at the battle of Adua. The Italians accepted their reverse, and signed treaties with the emperor in 1900, 1902 and 1908 establishing the border between their new colony of Eritrea and Ethiopia.

With the rise of fascism under Mussolini, Italy was determined to extend its presence in the Horn of Africa. Its invasion of Ethiopia in October 1935 was condemned by the League of Nations, but it was only with the outbreak of the Second

World War that the international community took a decisive stand against Italian aggression. By 1941 Emperor Haile Selassie had been returned to his throne by a combined force of British, South African, Indian and Sudanese troops fighting alongside Ethiopian patriots. While Ethiopia was independent once more, the international community was left with the problem of what to do with Eritrea, which was under temporary British military administration. It was not until 1952 that the United Nations finally decided that the territory should be federated with Ethiopia. There matters might have rested but for the absolutist rule of the emperor, who managed to alienate the population by a series of decrees outlawing the teaching of Eritrean languages, dismantling industries and removing them to Addis Ababa, and repressing the trade union movement and political parties allowed under the British.

By the early 1960s this repression was being met by armed resistance. Despite this, there was still considerable support inside Eritrea for unity with Ethiopia, particularly from among the Christian highlanders. In November 1962, after intense pressure from Addis Ababa, the federation was ended, and Eritrea was absorbed into Ethiopia. This served to spur on the opposition, led at first by the Eritrean Liberation Front (ELF), whose origins can partly be traced back to the Muslim League of the 1940s and which drew most of its support from the Muslim community. Disputes within the ELF, and particularly hostility towards Christian recruits, resulted in the formation of the Eritrean People's Liberation Front in the early 1970s. The EPLF rejected ethnic differences and stood for a secular and socialist state. An uneasy truce between the two ended in a bitter civil war which the EPLF finally won in 1981, forcing the ELF out of Eritrea.

Despite these divisions, Ethiopia's campaign against Eritrean self-determination did not go well. Discontent inside the Ethiopian army over the conduct of the war and the handling of a devastating famine led to the overthrow of the emperor in 1974. Haile Selassie was replaced by a committee – the Dergue – which came to be led by the equally autocratic Mengistu Haile Mariam. After initial discussions with the Eritreans failed, the war continued and intensified. But the events of 1974 led to a second, equally important development. Students from Tigray, angered by the lack of development of their province, and building on the ancient claims of Tigray to be the centre of the Ethiopian state, launched their own campaign to break Amhara rule. In 1975 the TPLF was formed, and began waging its own war against Addis Ababa.

Nationalism

On the face of it the EPLF and the TPLF had much in common, since they both opposed Ethiopian absolutism, whether exercised by Haile Selassie or by Mengistu Haile Mariam. In reality, however, the forms of national identity that the two movements pursued and in a sense embodied were very different. These differences were fundamental, and are probably the origin of much of the current conflict. The Eritreans saw their struggle as an anti-colonial movement fighting to regain a lost political independence. The Tigrayans, on the other hand, accepted that they were part of the Ethiopian empire in which their rightful place was exemplified by the fact that there had been a Tigrayan emperor, Johannes IV. They regarded the Mengistu regime as an oppressive state and believed that they had the right to self-determination up to and including independence from it.

An Eritrean identity was more complex and more difficult to forge precisely because it reflected a more diverse population. Eritrea's 3.5 million people are divided between two major religions and speak nine different languages. The Christian agriculturalists of the central highlands share a common language, religion and ethnic background with the mainly Tigrinya-speaking population inside the Ethiopian region of Tigray, south of the Mereb river. Intermarriage between Tigrinya speakers of Eritrea and Tigray was common. As an Eritrean put it in 1994, 'Tigrayans are our brethren, part of our soul'.

These areas had historically been part of the Ethiopian empire; the mainly Muslim lowland pastoralists, on the other hand, who live to the west, north and east of the highlands have little in common with them. The lowlanders' support for the ELF was predominantly motivated by a sense of alienation from a highland government, speaking a different language and espousing a different religion. The first decade of the armed struggle, from 1961 to 1974, was largely confined to the Muslim lowlands, and driven more by this sense of alienation than by a positive sense of Eritrean nationalism.

The EPLF attempted to mobilize Eritrean opinion irrespective of religion, but came up against considerable difficulties. Not all the Christians in the highlands supported the cause, and as late as 1982 some were still willing to act as armed militia for the Ethiopian administration. Outside the highlands, despite the terror employed by the Mengistu regime, a majority within the Kunama and the Afar peoples were at best ambivalent about the EPLF, while some actually supported continued unity with Ethiopia. As a result the EPLF had to conduct a vigorous campaign within its own community to win their support or acquiescence.

While the movement recognized and even celebrated the ethnic diversity of Eritrea, it resolutely refused to allow ethnicity to undermine its campaign for an independent state. This is not to suggest that ethnicity did not play any part in the front's activities; great care was taken to represent the whole of the population within the leadership, even when they were not as well represented among its membership. The EPLF also spent a good deal of time and effort inculcating a wider sense of Eritrean identity in its new recruits.

4

For the TPLF mobilization in Tigray was relatively simple, since it could call upon an existing concept of Tigrayan nationalism, a common history of oppression and a shared myth of the past common to all the areas in which it operated. Tigrayans shared a common language, religion and mode of livelihood. The TPLF's activities were an attempt to end Amhara rule. In Tigrayan eyes the Amhara had usurped the traditional power base of Ethiopian society, and transferred it from the ancient Tigrayan capital of Axum to Addis Ababa. In its first political programme the organization specified that it was fighting for the independence of Tigray from Ethiopia. Shortly thereafter the manifesto was repudiated by a TPLF congress, but it was not publicly disowned for some time. This has been a recurrent issue for the movement, and has also been seized upon by its critics.[1]

Since the TPLF's war aims, at least in the beginning, centred on achieving power in Tigray itself, its successes against the forces of the Dergue posed something of a problem for the movement, and led to considerable internal debate. Would the movement be satisfied with capturing Tigray, or would a hostile government in Addis Ababa require them to fight for the control of all Ethiopia? By early 1989 the TPLF exercised almost total control over the Tigrayan countryside, and was having increasing success against Ethiopian troops in garrisons across the province. In February 1989 TPLF forces, bolstered by an EPLF armoured brigade, took the area around Endaselasie, in western Tigray. Within two weeks garrisoned towns across the province were abandoned, usually without a fight.

The TPLF had achieved its initial objectives, and held most of Tigray. The question now was whether to press on to Addis Ababa. The movement had by this time established the Ethiopian People's Revolutionary Democratic Front (EPRDF), together with a number of other Ethiopian organizations, with the aim of taking power in Addis Ababa. Its leadership had ambitions to rule the whole of Ethiopia but was frustrated by many of its own supporters who, to use Lenin's famous phrase, voted with their feet. Some 10,000 TPLF fighters spontaneously returned home.[2]

Only after months of protracted discussion was the leadership able to convince its followers that they should continue prosecuting the war. Tigrayan nationalism was, at least for the time being, to be subordinated within a wider Ethiopian identity.

The EPLF and the TPLF relied, therefore, upon completely different nationalisms. The Eritrean struggle, from 1961, generated a powerful sense of collective identity, as did the increasingly genocidal responses of the Dergue towards Tigrayans and Eritreans during the 1980s. It was a nationalism forged in blood and with a clear

[1] John Young, *Peasant Revolution in Ethiopia* (Cambridge: Cambridge University Press, 1997), pp. 99–100.
[2] John Young, 'The Tigray People's Liberation Front', in Christopher Clapham (ed.), *African Guerrillas* (London: James Currey, 1998), p. 48.

objective in mind, namely an independent Eritrea.[3] Moreover, it was a nationalism that could justly claim to have been shaped by its own experience of colonialism. Italian rule had fashioned Eritrea just as other European colonizers had brought into being the other states of the continent, after the scramble for Africa at the end of the nineteenth century. Moreover, Italian colonialism had brought with it some of the benefits of European rule, in the shape of modern port facilities, roads and railways. The city of Asmara had developed into a pleasant town, with coffee shops, an opera house and fine government buildings. Eritrea also had political parties and a labour movement, none of which were to be found across the border. By the time the Italians were driven out by the Allied forces in 1941, they left behind a far more developed state than the feudal empire that existed in Ethiopia.

The Tigrayans also had much to be proud of. They could call on a historic past, on the rule of the last 'Tigrayan' emperor and a history of rebellions against imperial rule. The most important of these was the '*woyane*' rebellion of 1943 against Haile Selassie, from which the TPLF took its inspiration. But while Eritrean nationalism was clearly associated with a nation-state, Tigrayan nationalism had to play a difficult balancing act, recognizing the aspirations of the Tigrayan people but within the framework of the wider Ethiopian state. It was a problem that was to dog the relationship between the TPLF and the EPLF.

A troubled cooperation

Opposition to the dictatorial rule exercised from Addis Ababa united the two liberation movements, but a number of factors, including ideology, tactics and alliances, divided them. Over time these grew in importance.

In 1974 as the founders of the TPLF were preparing to launch an armed struggle, they made contact with the Eritrean movements, the obvious place to go for assistance. They sought support from the EPLF rather than the ELF, in part as a reaction to the fact that another group of Tigrayans had already set up the Tigray Liberation Front (TLF) in 1972–3 and formed an alliance with the ELF, receiving arms and training. From the EPLF they obtained promises of military training as well as arms and, significantly, two EPLF veterans, Mahari Haile (who took the field

---

[3] The difficulty for the EPLF was that the original cradle of the liberation movement was the Muslim pastoral areas to the north and west of Asmara. EPLF support came primarily from the Kebessa, the central Tigrayan-inhabited Christian agricultural areas of Eritrea – Akele Guzai, Serae and Hamasien regions. These had previously been an integral part of Ethiopia, sharing culture, history, language, religion and ethnicity with Tigray. The people of the Kebessa were slow to support the independence struggle against the Ethiopian government. The major factor, in the end, was the failure of the Ethiopian regime to produce an acceptable administration. See Alemseged Abbay, *Identity Jilted or Re-imagining Identity?* (New Jersey: Red Sea Press, 1998); Tekeste Negash, *No Medicine for the Bite of a White Snake: Notes on Nationalism and Resistance in Eritrea, 1890–1940* (University of Uppsala, 1986).

name 'Mussie' and went on to be the first military commander) and Yemane Kidane (who took the name 'Jamaica'), a member of the present Ethiopian government. The first group of TPLF trainees, twenty in all, was sent to Eritrea at the same time.

This cooperation was fruitful and they learned much from the Eritreans. However, not all of it was to their liking. Ideology came to play a significant part in their differences. On the face of it, both shared a Marxist analysis. In reality this was more of an impediment than a spur to unity. The EPLF's Marxism tended to be mainly 'Third Worldist' – long on anti-imperialist rhetoric and slogans. It regarded the Soviet bloc as 'strategic allies', even though they never received direct assistance from Moscow. States in the region that were close to the Soviet Union, such as South Yemen, did provide some training and support in the initial stages, but this disappeared after the Dergue seized power in 1974.

The TPLF, on the other hand, was influenced by Maoism, and admired Albania as an example of an anti-Soviet socialist state. In the early 1980s Meles Zenawi rose to authority in the movement, and in 1984 the Marxist Leninist League of Tigray was formed, as a vanguard party within the TPLF. The MLLT established links with Eritrean Marxist groups, notably the Democratic Movement, later the Democratic Movement for the Liberation of Eritrea. The Democratic Movement, itself a faction of the ELF (which broke apart after its defeat by the EPLF in 1981), was allowed to continue to have bases in the Tigray region until about 1996, much to the annoyance of the EPLF.

The United States had openly backed the emperor, Haile Selassie, but his fall and the assumption of power by the Dergue led to a change in international support. Now it was Moscow, rather than Washington, that backed Ethiopia. This change tested the Eritreans' position to the full, but they still resisted labelling the Soviet Union as imperialist, realizing that they might one day need its support as a permanent member of the Security Council if they were to finally achieve United Nations recognition of an independent Eritrea.[4] The Tigrayans had no such difficulties, and had no hesitation in condemning the Soviet Union as imperialist. Arcane as such arguments may now seem, they were an important source of friction between the two movements.[5]

Ideology was not the only issue to divide the movements. There was also the question of military tactics. While the TPLF's military strategy was one of mobile

[4] In August 1977, the EPLF summed up its position thus: 'The democratic forces of the Eritrean revolution led by the EPLF, while criticising and opposing the erroneous stands and baseless slanders of the socialist countries and democratic forces, have not wavered from its principled solidarity and alliances with these strategic friends'. ('The present political situation', Memorandum, August 1978, in EPLF, *Selected Articles from EPLF Publications (1973–1980)*, May 1982, p. 44.)
[5] See John Young, 'The Tigray and Eritrean Liberation Fronts: A History of Tensions and Pragmatism', *Journal of Modern African Studies*, 34, 1 (1996), p. 115.

guerrilla warfare, the EPLF combined mobile with fixed positional warfare, based on a securely defended rear area. In this base area they established a considerable infrastructure, including schools, hospitals and workshops. As the Eritreans moved towards more conventional forms of warfare, the Tigrayans became increasingly critical of their tactics.

Matters came to a head during the 'Red Star' campaign mounted by Ethiopia in 1982. It was the most sustained offensive the government forces were ever to undertake, and came within an ace of capturing the EPLF's base area, and with it Nakfa, the last town in rebel hands. Tigrayan fighters training with the EPLF were called upon to go into action, apparently without the permission of the TPLF central committee, who were furious at not being asked. After heroic efforts their combined forces just managed to repel the Ethiopian onslaught. Casualties were heavy, however, and the TPLF was deeply critical of the tactics employed by the EPLF, accusing it of moving too rapidly from guerrilla warfare to positional encounters with the enemy.

According to senior members of the TPLF, the Eritreans wanted TPLF fighters to remain in Eritrea to assist in defending Eritrean positions. By this time, however, the TPLF leadership was determined to overthrow the government in Addis Ababa. Its strategy, therefore, was to make alliances with other Ethiopian opposition movements and to take the military struggle south to the gates of the capital. It therefore withdrew its fighters from Eritrea. This did nothing to endear it to its allies, but worse was to follow.

In the mid-1980s these differences culminated in a public exchange of insults: the EPLF was defined as 'social imperialist' by the TPLF. The EPLF in turn labelled the TPLF 'childish'. This masked a serious theoretical difference with major political ramifications for the national question in Ethiopia.[6] The issue was originally whether or not self-determination should be taken as far as secession. It was a critical question for the student radicals in Addis Ababa in the 1960s and 1970s, many of whom went on to lead the Eritrean and Tigrayan liberation movements. The TPLF recognized Eritrea's unique status as a former colonial state. But they also came to promote the right to secession of the various nationalities within Ethiopia and – far more controversially – of those within Eritrea as well. During its exchange of polemics with the EPLF in 1986/7, the TPLF even stated that 'a truly democratic' Eritrea would have to respect 'the right of its own nationalities up to and including secession'.[7]

This infuriated and appalled the EPLF, which stated that it was precisely because Eritrea was a former colonial state that it had the right to independence. Its response was to argue that Ethiopian nationalities had a right to self-determination, but not to

[6] See M. Duffield, and J. Prendergast, *Without Troops and Tanks: Humanitarian Intervention in Ethiopia and Eritrea* (New Jersey: Red Sea Press, 1994), p. 100.
[7] *People's Voice* (1986), Special Issue.

independence, as this was conditional on a colonial experience.[8] The EPLF was well aware that any widening of the definition of self-determination to include independence would detract from Eritrea's special status as a colonially defined territory. Moreover, giving Eritrean nationalities rights to secede would also jeopardize the future cohesion of Eritrea, not least because both the Tigrayan and Afar peoples live on both sides of the border.

The TPLF believed that the EPLF's refusal to recognize the right of its own nationalities to secede was an example of its undemocratic nature. For this reason the TPLF came to regard its relationship with the EPLF as tactical, rather than enduring, and consequently the TPLF went on to provide support to other Eritrean movements, such as the Democratic Marxist League of Eritrea, which they found more ideologically acceptable. According to EPLF documents, the TPLF's flirtation with other movements came as a surprise and a disappointment and led to a rupture in their alliance.

> [T]he TPLF had concluded that the EPLF was not a democratic organization and that its relationship with the EPLF was 'tactical'. The EPLF had thought that its cooperation with the TPLF was genuine and not based on temporary tactical considerations. And so, when the TPLF's secret stand became public the EPLF realised its naiveté and although it did not regret its past actions, decided to break its relationship with the TPLF and not enter into polemics with it.[9]

The EPLF decided to teach the TPLF a brutal lesson in power politics. The Eritreans closed the TPLF's radio station, which had been operating from EPLF-controlled territory. More importantly, in June 1985, at the height of the famine that was then devastating the Horn of Africa, the EPLF cut the TPLF's supply lines to Sudan. It did this by closing the road which passed through Eritrea, thereby denying the Tigrayan people access to food aid at a crucial juncture. It was a drastic measure indeed. Although nothing was said in public at the time, it is not hard to imagine the animosity that this generated. The TPLF responded with characteristic efficiency, mobilizing 100,000 peasants to drive an alternative route to Sudan that did not go via Eritrea.

While the EPLF leadership still refuses to speak about these events, Tigrayans remember them with considerable bitterness. As one put it: 'The EPLF behaviour was a savage act ... I do not hesitate to categorise it as a "savage act". It must be recorded in history like that!'[10]

[8] *Adulis* (May 1985).

[9] *EPLF Political Report and NDP* (March 1987), pp. 148–9; quoted in Young, 'The Tigray and Eritrean People's Liberation Fronts', p. 115.

[10] Tekleweini Assefa, Head of the Relief Society of Tigray, interviewed in Abbay, *Identity Jilted or Re-imagining Identity?*, p. 129.

Despite this rupture, the imperatives of war continued to drive the two movements back into each other's arms. By 1987 both fronts had won considerable military victories, but realized that further advances required cooperation. In April 1988, after four days of discussions in Khartoum, a joint statement was issued, indicating that their differences had been overcome. It was at this time that the Tigrayans suggested that the Ethiopian–Eritrean border should be demarcated. The Eritreans persuaded them to postpone this until after the defeat of the Ethiopian regime. It was to prove a crucial mistake. Yet at the time it seemed insignificant, and from then until the overthrow of the Mengistu regime, the TPLF and EPLF were allies once more.

Military cooperation led to military success. By the time the Eritreans finally took Asmara in May 1991 and the Ethiopians marched into Addis Ababa, supported by EPLF units, the movements had forged strong bonds. Their members had fought side by side against appalling odds, while their leaderships had come to know, trust and rely upon one another. Differences remained, but there appeared every chance that these could be overcome, given the goodwill that existed. Agreements were made in 1991 and 1993 allowing for the free movement of labour, for Eritrea's use of Ethiopian currency, the birr, for regulated Ethiopian use of the port of Assab to minimize the effects of its loss of a coastline, and so on.

Indeed, cooperation between the two governing parties was so strong that a senior Eritrean could seriously look forward to the day when the two countries were united once more in a federal structure.[11] Extraordinary as such sentiments might seem today, they genuinely reflected the optimism of the time.

[11] Amare Tekle (ed.), *Eritrea and Ethiopia: From Conflict to Co-operation* (New Jersey: Red Sea Press, 1994), p. 17.

3 BEHIND THE CONFLICT

Initial difficulties

Even at the moment of victory, cracks were appearing in the relationship between the EPLF and TPLF. The EPLF not only expelled from its soil the Ethiopian army of occupation, it insisted that tens of thousands of Ethiopian citizens who had been involved in the Ethiopian administration leave as well. Between 1991 and 1992 around 120,000 Ethiopians were forced to go. The majority were members of the defeated Ethiopian army, but a good number were not, having worked in Eritrea all their lives, and many knew no other home. One expelled Ethiopian complained: 'The Eritrean soldiers told us we were strangers. But I was born in Eritrea like everyone else in my family.'[12] Those expelled were not allowed to take their possessions and some had to abandon houses, businesses and cars.

Eritrean-born women who had married or cohabited with civil servants and soldiers from other parts of Ethiopia, with their children, formed a significant number of those deported. It was made clear that 'collaborators' of this kind were considered traitors, and many of those who were not expelled suffered social ostracism. The newly installed Ethiopian government neither officially complained nor retaliated.[13] It continued to allow up to half a million Ethiopians of Eritrean origin to live inside Ethiopia. Reportedly, the Eritrean community inside Addis Ababa had been one of the most reliable sources of intelligence for the EPRDF when it took the capital.

The circumstances surrounding the victory threw up their own difficulties. Eritrean support for the Tigrayans in capturing Addis Ababa was seen as a sign by many Ethiopians that the TPLF was in the EPLF's pocket. This view was particularly prevalent among Amhara, whom the Tigrayans now displaced from power. Their accusation that Meles Zenawi was insufficiently pro-Ethiopian in his policies was a potential liability to the new prime minister. He could either be seen as failing to be robust enough in his defence of Ethiopian interests, or – from the perspective of the TPLF – insufficiently strong in prosecuting policies that favoured Tigray.

[12] *The Independent*, 25 July 1991.
[13] Eritrean officials account for this by saying that this purging of agents of the former government was a strategy worked out with the TPLF which carried out its own purge of Tigray.

The question of secession, referred to above, also served to drive the movements apart. Their views on the nature of the state were diametrically opposed. The new Ethiopian government reformed the state along ethnic lines. The new constitution of 1995 allowed for 'a voluntary union of the nationalities of Ethiopia', which included the right to secession.[14] By contrast, the Eritreans, building on their vision of their country as a product of colonialism, opted for a unitary state. The Eritrean constitution specifically forbids religious or ethnically based parties.

These differences can easily be overstated. Neither government has, in practice, tolerated much in the way of dissent. Political parties, other than the People's Front for Democracy and Justice – the successor to the EPLF – are not permitted to operate in Eritrea. Ethiopians may give their backing to any political movement, as long as it is sanctioned by the ruling Ethiopian People's Revolutionary Democratic Front. But the differences between them allowed the Ethiopians to continue to maintain links with Eritrean opposition movements.

Despite these tensions, the outward signs were that all was well between Addis Ababa and Asmara. Government delegations came and went, and life proceeded as normal. Yet relations between what were now the governments of Ethiopia and Eritrea were not put upon the kind of solid footing that would stand the strains of office. Part of the problem was the fact that Eritrea achieved *de facto* independence in May 1991, but this was not formalized until May 1993; for example, it was only then that the Joint Ministerial Consultative Committee was set up. However, a series of meetings on the border did take place, initiated by the local administration on each side of it.

Even after 1993 the leaderships of the two victorious movements continued to treat relations between their two countries as if they were relations between liberation movements or even between individuals. Hence the bureaucratic infrastructure that supports interstate relations was either not established or else sidelined. If President Afeworki had a serious issue that he wished to raise concerning Ethiopia he simply contacted Prime Minister Meles Zenawi, and vice versa.

This weakened the relations between the states in two crucial ways. First, it left plenty of scope for misinterpretation and recriminations. Second, it meant that if the relationships between individuals broke down, there was no official position to fall back upon. Even when committees were established, they operated with such informality that when challenged by the critical events that led to the recent clashes, they failed to function effectively.

---

[14] J. Abbink, 'Briefing: The Eritrea–Ethiopian Border Dispute', *African Affairs*, Vol. 97 (1998), p. 556.

Economic relations deteriorate

Economics also had a considerable part to play in souring what had been firm ties between the two states. Indeed, an examination of the economic issues is crucial to both the origins and the implications of the conflict. In terms of origins, economics was the only sphere of public disagreement between the authorities prior to the outbreak of hostilities. Until then relations between the two countries appeared to be remarkably good, with economic cooperation reinforcing the political ties that had been forged during the years preceding the overthrow of the Dergue. Open animosity over bilateral trade relations surfaced in late 1997 following Eritrea's introduction of its new currency, the nakfa. While apparently not a causal factor in the immediate crisis of mid-May 1998, the new currency and ensuing dispute over trade relations had three consequences.

First, the introduction of Eritrea's new currency necessitated a clear delineation of the border from mid-1997 in order to regulate cross-border trade, taxation and foreign exchange flows. Second, the new currency prompted a dispute at the end of 1997 over the precise nature of post-nakfa trade between Eritrea and Ethiopia, tarnishing relations between the two administrations in late 1997 and early 1998. Third, friction was exacerbated as the currency and trade dispute severely disrupted the flow of goods, remittances and labourers across the border, generating new political pressures on both Eritrean and Tigrayan leaderships. Taken together, these economic factors appear to have rekindled old animosities between the respective ruling groups, eroding their ability and willingness to compromise or negotiate over disagreements.

The most significant short-term economic consequence of the conflict was the suspension of all trade and communications links between Ethiopia and Eritrea. A *de facto* partial trade embargo was applied largely at Asmara's instigation in December 1997, following the dispute over the introduction of Eritrea's new currency. Nevertheless, normal air, road and telecommunications links all remained open. It was only in mid-May after the fighting at Badme that the rupture became total as the Ethiopian authorities precipitously suspended all links and decided to immediately halt the use of the ports of Massawa and Assab for foreign trade, which has since been channelled via Djibouti.

Alongside the logistical implications of this break in relations, the immediate cost of conflict can be seen in terms of the rapid rearmament and mobilization programmes undertaken by both sides. In addition to the immediate fiscal implications, this has a longer-term impact on economic planning, investment and thus future growth and poverty reduction. Such costs are relatively greater for Eritrea's far smaller, and structurally weaker, economy. However, in the Eritrean case these short-term costs appear to have been partly offset by a sharp increase in its main source of foreign exchange, remittances from Eritreans abroad.

The 1997 nakfa/birr currency dispute and bilateral trade

Between 1991 and 1997 Ethiopia and Eritrea operated a *de facto* currency union, using the Ethiopian birr. The National Bank of Ethiopia controlled monetary policy. While technically this diminished Eritrea's new-found sovereignty, in practice the Ethiopian government's tight monetary policy provided Eritrea with a stable reserve currency and risk-free trade with Ethiopia, which remained its largest market and supplier. Monetary stability in Eritrea was enhanced by the fact that the authorities in Asmara managed foreign exchange extremely pragmatically. By offering a slight premium over the dollar/birr rate prevailing in Ethiopia, they ensured that all remittances from Eritreans abroad flowed into the official banking system.

In 1992 the Eritrean authorities nevertheless stated that they would create their own national currency. In early 1997 they announced that the currency, to be known as the nakfa, would be in operation by the end of the year. Early in 1997 Asmara forwarded a series of suggestions about future trade relations to the Ethiopian authorities, and details of its phased introduction were announced in July. The Eritreans proposed retaining the 1:1 birr/nakfa parity and suggested that both currencies could circulate on either side of the border. The Ethiopian government turned this proposal down.

After what the Eritreans claim were eight months of procrastination, the Ethiopian government announced unilaterally in late October 1997 that instead of Eritrea's proposal for a fixed rate and dual currency arrangement, the two countries would have a normal, arm's-length trade regime. Trade would therefore be conducted as between any two sovereign states with separate currencies, via hard currency and letters of credit. The only exception was for petty cross-border trade, defined as goods with a value of under birr 2,000 (US$285), for which a licensing system and designated border posts were opened by Ethiopia.

It is clear from subsequent public statements that this decision came as a shock and a rebuff to the Eritreans. They clearly believed both that the dual currency regime would benefit Eritrea's economy and that the Ethiopians would acquiesce to this arrangement.[15]

The introduction of the nakfa was completed by December 1997. In October Ethiopia had simultaneously begun issuing a new set of Ethiopian birr bank notes, thus avoiding any potential 'leakage' back into Ethiopia of birr redeemed for nakfa in Eritrea. The newly designated birr notes also meant that the defunct iconography of the Mengistu era, notably patriotic slogans and a map of Ethiopia which incorporated Eritrea, were withdrawn from circulation. Ironically the new map only served to fuel suspicion between the two countries. After May 1998 Eritrean officials

---

[15] 'Interview with Tekie Beyene, head of the National Bank of Eritrea', *The Reporter*, Addis Ababa, 19 November 1997.

began claiming that Tigrayan 'expansionist ambitions' could be seen in the shape of the border incorporated into the tiny inset map on the newly designed birr notes.

Notwithstanding the trade dispute, by the time the border conflict erupted, the birr and nakfa appeared to be trading at almost identical rates (c. 7.05–7.20 to the US dollar). In early May the Eritrean authorities announced they would let the nakfa float, adding that they did not expect to have to intervene to maintain this rate.

Public perceptions

There is also a question of perception. The EPLF had given training and succour to the TPLF in its early stages, and tended to treat the movement as its 'younger brother'. Ordinary Tigrayans had long felt patronized by Eritreans. They had for many years taken low-paid, low-status jobs in Eritrea, as casual labourers and domestic servants. Tigrayans were denigrated as 'agame' – a term that implied they were all uncouth peasants.[16]

Ethiopians charged the Eritreans with wishing to industrialize at their expense, using Ethiopia only as a supplier of cheap labour and raw materials, and as a market for Eritrean exports.

There is also a cultural issue that is perhaps easily ignored. Neither Ethiopians nor Eritreans are given to clear, open communication. Secrecy, always a necessity for guerrilla movements, was almost turned into a cult during the war. Often this was required by the unfolding events. Eritreans, for example, insisted that all recruits take a *nom de guerre*, and forbade all discussion of family and origins. This was vital, given that the entire Eritrean population numbered around three million people, and it would have been all too easy to extract information that might have endangered families still living behind enemy lines. This secrecy was not easily abandoned once the exigencies of war were at an end. While it may have served both movements well during the years of turmoil, it allowed misunderstandings to multiply and rumour to replace open debate that might have resolved genuine differences.

Finally, it is important not to ignore another accretion of the long years of struggle. Both movements and both leaderships were hardened by battle. They developed a resolution that saw them through the most difficult of times. They inculcated in all involved a determination to press ahead, no matter what the cost. Anything less than a steely will was seen as a sign of weakness. Finding compromises in this climate was no easy task.

None of these issues were insurmountable, however. Given time and patience, they could and probably would have been resolved. But far from being removed,

---

[16] The term is derived from the name of one of the poorest areas of Tigray, which abuts onto Eritrea.

during the years 1991 to 1998 differences were allowed to accumulate. Some analysts who knew both sides well warned that there could be trouble in store. John Young predicted as early as 1996 that 'political differences between the TPLF and the EPLF during their years of struggle will be reflected in their present and future relations, and as a result they may be far more problematic than is generally imagined'.[17]

When the events of May 1998 unfolded, the old differences, compounded by the weaknesses and irritations that had emerged after 1991, turned former friends into bitter adversaries.

---

[17] Young, 'The Tigray and Eritrean People's Liberation Fronts', p. 120.

4 THE FIRST BLOWS

There is absolutely no agreement between the two countries about what set off the current conflict. All that is clear is that it was the culmination of many underlying tensions. As Ethiopian Prime Minister Meles Zenawi put it, the incident was 'Sarajevo, 1914. It was an accident waiting to happen.'[18]

What is agreed is that the clash on 6 May 1998 took place in the area around Badme. Both countries lay claim to this area between the Meret and Tekezze rivers, one of several disputed sections of their 1,000-kilometre-long border, the others being Humera in the west, close to the border with Sudan; Tserona and Zalembessa north of Adigrat; Alitiena and Irob; Bada in the northern Dankalia depression and Bure on the road to Assab.

The situation in each of these contested areas is complex, and maps and historical background can only provide an indication of how they might be resolved. The area around Alitiena is illustrative. It is certainly shown on most maps as a part of Eritrea, but it is also usually identified as part of the district of Irob. Irob has always been administered from Ethiopia. The three main lineages in Irob are largely Christian, though they have at times paid tribute and taxes to the Afar sultans. They consider themselves to be Tigrayans. Irob has some significance because of its salt, which is exported through Eritrea, and also because of its position. Whoever controls Irob can dominate Bada, which has the best land and water in the northern depression. To complicate the issue, this is an area of interest to the Afar Revolutionary Democratic United Front which has been, and still is, fighting for the unity of Afars of Ethiopia and Eritrea, within Ethiopia. This is a strategy which brings it into conflict with both governments.

The area around Badme is equally complex. When the border was defined by the international agreements after the defeat of Italian troops by Ethiopian forces in 1896, the Badme region was sparsely populated. Over time Eritrean and Tigrayan farmers came to settle it, joining the Kunama who had originally lived there. In the 1960s the Ethiopian administrator of Tigray was Ras Mengesha – properly Ras Mengesh Seyoum, governor of Tigray region and its hereditary ruler, a grandson of

---

[18] *The Economist*, 8 May 1999, p. 74.

Emperor Yohannis IV. He paid little attention to the area, and allowed the development of agricultural settlements on both sides of the border. These were administered by the Tigrayan district of Shire. This made little difference, since after the United Nations federated Eritrea with Ethiopia in 1952, the border had little relevance. After Eritrea's autonomy was ended in 1961 it became no more than an internal Ethiopian provincial border. Essentially, therefore, the main area now under dispute, around Badme, was administered by Tigray, irrespective of which side of the line it fell.[19]

The area was not particularly fertile ground for the EPLF. The Kunama were, historically, resistant to the idea of an independent Eritrea, and fought for the Ethiopian government against the ELF and the EPLF during the war. When the area finally fell to the EPLF in 1991, a significant number of Kunama fled to Axum inside Ethiopia, fearing reprisals. Moreover, the area was traditionally an ELF, rather than an EPLF, area of operation. When the ELF were ousted from Eritrea in 1981 by the EPLF, with TPLF help, it was the Tigrayans who took over in the Badme area, establishing Sheraro as a major base. The Tigrayans continued to administer the area after 1991, just as the EPLF claims it administered other pockets of territory that fell within Ethiopia. Given the warm relations between the two governments at the time, it appeared to make little difference, and both had more pressing tasks to attend to as they consolidated their hold on their respective countries.

After 1991 occasional disputes occurred along the entire Ethiopia–Eritrea border. Most were local and small-scale. According to Eritrean sources, they were the sort of conflicts that flare up along any ill-defined border which is straddled by farming communities. Frequently these took place during the ploughing season, as farmers clashed over the exact boundaries of their fields. Low-level meetings between local officials took place in an attempt to resolve these matters. According to the Eritreans, no fewer than six such meetings took place between November 1993 and March 1996.[20] When these meetings failed to resolve matters a further series of discussions was held, this time involving senior party officials at a regional level. Again these failed to produce the desired results, apparently because the Ethiopian representatives claimed that the permanent boundary should be the *de facto* line convened in 1987 between the TPLF and ELF, which included six small Eritrean villages in Ethiopia.[21] Following a more serious conflict over the Bada area of southern Eritrea in 1997, President Isaais Afeworki wrote to Prime Minister Meles Zenawi on 25 August of that year, proposing that a Joint Border Commission be set

---

[19] Jean-Louis Peninou, 'The Ethiopian–Eritrean Border Conflict', *IBRU Boundary and Security Bulletin*, Summer 1998, pp. 46–50.
[20] Network of Eritrean Professionals in Europe, *A War Without Cause* (London 1998), p. 5.
[21] Peninou, 'The European–Eritrean Boarder Conflict', p. 48.

18

up at governmental level.[22] Ethiopia presents a rather different picture, maintaining that the initiative for establishing the Commission came from its side, following a deterioration in relations 'as a consequence of economic issues'.[23]

The first meeting of the Commission took place in Asmara on 13 November 1997. The Eritrean side evidently pressed for a speedy resolution of the border issue, given the deteriorating situation on the ground. According to Ethiopia, a common understanding was reached at the meeting:

- to assign a technical sub-committee drawn from both countries to examine the border question and to report to the commission to be formed;
- that each party should declare to the other side the list of its members to be represented in the sub-committee;
- that both sides respect the status quo and take measures to alleviate impending border disputes until such time as a lasting solution was attained.[24]

However, no further meeting took place until 8 May 1998, with the Eritreans blaming Ethiopian procrastination for the delay.

In the meantime an apparently minor, unrelated event occurred that convinced the Eritrean government that the Tigrayans were up to no good. The German government aid agency, the GTZ, operates in three regions of Ethiopia. Early in 1997 the GTZ was approached by the Regional Education Board of Tigray. It was asked to help fund the printing of a new map of Tigray for distribution to primary schools. It agreed to do so, and 1,000 maps were duly printed, with the GTZ logo at the bottom. The map turned out to be deeply controversial, for it portrayed the border with Eritrea in a completely new light. Several areas that had been the subject of the heated discussions between the two countries were now shown as being part of Tigray. For the Eritreans this was proof positive of the hostile intentions of the Tigrayans. Some interpreted it as the result of the long-held TPLF dream of a 'Greater Tigray', that would take in all Tigrayan speakers, as outlined in the TPLF manifesto of 1976.[25]

The German government was horrified to be caught up in this controversy. It came in for considerable criticism, both in the Horn and in the German parliament, where several MPs support the Eritrean cause. The GTZ insists that all it did was help finance the project, and it had no responsibility whatsoever for the contents of the map, which was drawn up by the Ethiopian Mapping Authority.

It was against this background that a high-level delegation left Asmara on 7 May 1998 for the meeting of the Border Commission the following day. Led by Defence

[22] Network of Eritrean Professionals in Europe, *A War Without Cause*, p. 8.
[23] Ethiopian Foreign Ministry statement, 12 August 1998.
[24] Ibid.
[25] Network of Eritrean Professionals in Europe, *A War Without Cause*, pp. 10–11.

Minister Sebhat Efrem, it was *en route* to Addis Ababa when the first incident took place. Both sides say the meeting on the 8th went well. According to the Ethiopians it was agreed that two members of the Joint Commission would meet in Asmara in a month's time to hammer out an agreement and report back to the larger group. They say that it was further agreed that Eritrean armed units which had crossed into Ethiopian territory since 6 May would withdraw to Eritrea and that the *status quo ante* would prevail until a final agreement had been reached.[26] At the end of the meeting the group agreed to meet again early the following day, but when the Ethiopians arrived to pick up their guests, they discovered that the Eritreans had checked out of their hotel and flown back to Asmara.

There then followed three days of intensive discussions over the telephone between senior leaders on both sides. These proved fruitless, with each side blaming the other for the failure to resolve the growing crisis. On the morning of 12 May Eritrean troops backed by tanks took Badme town and its environs. The following day the Ethiopian parliament passed a resolution condemning the Eritrean 'aggression', demanding an immediate and unconditional withdrawal of Eritrean forces and warning that Ethiopia reserved the right to defend its territorial integrity and sovereignty. Ethiopian troop reinforcements were sent to the border. Exactly what happened subsequently is the subject of very different interpretations.

[26] Ethiopian Ministry of Foreign Affairs, *Background to and Chronology of Events on the Eritrean Aggression against Ethiopia*, 24 June 1998.

5 CONFLICTING REALITIES

The view from Asmara

The official description of events was given in a press release from the Eritrean Ministry of Foreign Affairs dated 19 June 1998, entitled 'Background to the Current Border Dispute Between Eritrea and Ethiopia':

1. The crisis between Eritrea and Ethiopia is rooted in the violation by the government of Ethiopia of Eritrea's colonial boundaries, and its decision to wilfully claim, as well as physically occupy, large swathes of Eritrean territory in the southwestern, southern and southeastern parts of the country. This violation is made manifest in the official map issued in 1997 as well as the map of Ethiopia embossed in the new currency notes of the country that came into circulation in November 1997.

2. Ethiopia went further than laying claims on paper to create a *de facto* situation on the ground. The first forcible act of creating facts on the ground occurred in July 1997 when Ethiopia, under the pretext of fighting the Afar opposition, brought two battalions to Bada (Adi Murug) in southwestern Eritrea to occupy the village and dismantle the Eritrean administration there. This unexpected development was a cause of much concern to the government of Eritrea. Eritrea's Head of State subsequently sent a letter to the Ethiopian Prime Minister on 16 August 1997, reminding him that 'the forcible occupation of Adi Murug' was 'truly saddening'. He further urged him to 'personally take the necessary prudent action so that the measure that has been taken will not trigger unnecessary conflict'.[27] A week later, on 25 August 1997, the Eritrean Head of State again wrote to the Prime Minister stressing that measures similar to those in Bada were taken in the Badme (southwestern Eritrea) area and suggesting that a Joint Commission be set up to help check further deterioration and create a mechanism to resolve the problem.

[27] The letter, as released by the Eritreans, contains the following paragraph, which indicates how little concern the dispute caused at the time: 'It cannot be said that the border between our two countries is demarcated clearly although it is known traditionally. And we had not given the issue much attention in view of our present and future ties. Moreover, I do not believe that this will be a cause of much concern and controversy even in the future.' (Eritrean Foreign Ministry, 4 May 1999.)

3.   Unfortunately, Eritrean efforts to solve the problem amicably and bilaterally failed as the government of Ethiopia continued to bring under its occupation the Eritrean territories that it had incorporated into its map. Our worst fears were to be realized when, on 6 May 1998, on the eve of the second meeting of the Joint Border Commission, the Ethiopian army launched an unexpected attack on Eritrean armed patrols in the Badme area claiming that they had transgressed on areas that Ethiopia had newly brought under its control. This incident led to a series of clashes which, coupled with the hostile measures that were taken by the government of Ethiopia, resulted in the present state of war between the two countries.

4.   Ethiopia's unilateral redrawing of the colonial boundary and flagrant acts of creating facts on the ground are the essential causes of the current crisis. In the light of these facts, Ethiopia's claims that it is the victim of aggression are obviously false and meant to deceive the international community. Indeed, Ethiopia to this day occupies Eritrean territories in the Setit area in the south-western part of the country.

The statement then went on the claim that the Ethiopian action was a violation of the OAU Charter, and then proceeded to outline how the crisis might be resolved.

Informal discussions produce a more comprehensive Eritrean view. This is perhaps best summed up by the assertion by a senior Eritrean diplomat that the events that preceded the crisis were far more important than the events of May themselves. 'It's as if someone has been pinching you under the table for ages and you try to ignore it. Finally you can't any longer and you slap them in the face. Everyone sees the slap in the face, but no one knows about the pinching that preceded it.'

The Eritreans accept that there can be no walls between Eritrea and Ethiopia. There are some villages in Tigray wholly inhabited by Eritreans and vice versa. During the 1980s there was fighting between the ELF and the TPLF over where the border was, but the EPLF took the view that these quarrels were ridiculous while the Dergue was the principal enemy and that it was an issue that could easily be resolved later on. In any event, in their view, the maps and relevant treaties were absolutely clear about where the border lies.

Much to the surprise of the Eritreans the smouldering conflicts along the border grew in intensity over time. This they put down to splits within the TPLF, and in particular to the growing strength of militant Tigrayan nationalists within the MLLT. According to the Eritreans, Prime Minister Meles Zenawi had managed to gain the upper hand within the TPLF after the victories in 1988. It was his success within the movement that allowed him to sign the agreement in Khartoum in April of that year that paved the way for a resumption of cooperation with the EPLF.

22

The Eritrean view is that after both parties took power in 1991, Meles dispatched the most militant members of the TPLF, most of whom were in the MLLT, to Tigray. This was a major mistake, for the militants used their base within Tigray to plot against the Prime Minister. In particular they accused him of weakness in his dealings with Eritrea. As the national army was demobilized this faction was strengthened by the return of fighters to Tigray, many of whom joined the local militia. These militia, who were in some instances more powerful than the Ethiopian army itself, took a militant line, particularly with Eritrean villagers along the border. They began pushing Eritrean peasants out of the Badme area. A number of meetings were held to discuss this, with Eritrean officials asking what was going on. The Ethiopians responded by claiming that the villagers on the Eritrean side had been destroying their crops.

According to Asmara, by 1998 the situation on the border had deteriorated considerably, with local people informing Eritrean military units in the Gash Setit area that the Tigrayan administration was marking the border with stones 40–50 kilometres inside Eritrean territory. When they went to investigate they were met with a superior force which accused them of being inside Ethiopian territory and instructed them to disarm or be shot. They were surrounded, and in the ensuing gunfire four Eritrean soldiers were killed, including a senior officer.

The survivors got back to their base and reported what had taken place. The military were outraged. A BBC reporter in Asmara recounts: 'As one general told me, banging his fist on the desk in his office: "To die on the battlefield is one thing, there is honour, but to be killed in cold blood is completely unacceptable. They must be punished."'[28]

Up to this point everything might have been resolved, in the last instance, by Isaais Afeworki and Meles Zenawi. Once the conflict became public the crisis gained a momentum of its own. But the key to all of this, from the Eritrean point of view, is the weakness of the Ethiopian Prime Minister. All this might have been avoided, they say, had he not been under pressure from Tigrayan hard-liners, determined to establish the 'Greater Tigray' that has been at the heart of their project ever since the TPLF was founded in the 1970s. The implementation of this was to be achieved in two phases. The first involved the redrawing of the internal boundaries of Ethiopia to enlarge Tigray; this has already taken place. The second phase is the incorporation of areas of Eritrea within the borders of Tigray.[29] This is, in Eritrean eyes, behind every current development, and confirmed by documents found on Ethiopian prisoners of war.

[28] Alex Last, *Focus on Africa Magazine*, October–December 1998, p. 22.
[29] 'The ultimate aim of the TPLF leadership is the establishment of "Greater Tigray" with the Eritrean port of Assab as a capital city. The establishment of a "Republic of Greater Tigray" is the centerpiece of the TPLF's political programme' (Network of Eritrean Professionals in Europe, *A War Without Cause,* p. 10).

The view from Addis Ababa

The Ethiopian position was outlined by Prime Minister Meles Zenawi in an interview with Ethiopian journalists on 21 May 1998, when he insisted that he had no satisfactory explanation for why relations had deteriorated to the point of conflict.[30]

> I really cannot make head or tail of this puzzling development. In fact I may have my own guesses, but they cannot be satisfactory. As you all know, there were certain misunderstandings between the two governments arising from measures taken after changes in the currency on both sides. There were more or less certain misunderstandings even before this change, but it is very difficult for me to believe that the composite effect of all this would draw us into open conflict. That is why I still maintain I have no satisfactory answer to this baffling question.

Meles said the Badme area 'had never been, even for one day, under the jurisdiction of Eritrea – be it during the Italian occupation, under the British protectorate, at the time of the Federation or thereafter'. The Prime Minister also gave an account of the original incident.

> Some Eritrean armed men crossed our border and entered a locality called Badme. Our policemen approached them and told them to withdraw peacefully or put down their guns and conduct their business, if they had any, and then return to where they came from. But the Eritrean armed men began to claim that Badme is part of Eritrea and that Ethiopian policemen had no mandate to allow or forbid Eritreans from leaving or entering Badme. As the row intensified, they opened fire and inflicted casualties on the Ethiopian policemen.
>
> In the meantime we received information that Eritrean forces were surrounding Badme from various directions. Incidentally, the Joint Commission, which was dealing with border disputes, was due to convene here in Addis Ababa. When the Commission convened, we discussed the issue with the Eritrean delegation and reached a consensus on three major points. First, it was agreed by both sides to stay in their respective territories prior to the conflict until the dispute is settled peacefully. They also agreed to pull out Eritrean troops from the occupied territory. Second, both parties agreed to meet after two months to come up with the final framework for resolving border conflicts. Third, both parties reached an understanding to jointly investigate which side started the Badme conflict as there were conflicting reports from both sides. The Eritrean delegation led by the Minister of Defence left for Asmara the following Sunday, 10 May. We assumed that they would withdraw their troops. Contrary to our expectation, reports reached us that the Eritrean government was sending more troops to the disputed areas.

---

[30] Ethiopian television, Addis Ababa, Amharic, 21 May 1998; BBC Monitoring Service, 22 May 1998.

Then we sent a note of protest through their embassy against the Eritrean military build-up in the area, which clearly contravened the agreement we had reached earlier. We repeated our request for the withdrawal of Eritrean troops from the occupied Ethiopian territories.

Unfortunately, their response was not positive. Instead, they proposed third-party involvement to mediate the dispute. We did not oppose the idea but made it clear the occupation forces should withdraw first in accordance with the agreement reached earlier by both parties before any peaceful negotiation starts. On the contrary, they preferred to go ahead with sending more troops to the areas. On Monday, 11 May I could not get any response because I was told President Isaais was on a state visit to Saudi Arabia. The following day, 12 May, Eritrean government troops invaded Badme and part of Sheraro *woredas* [districts] backed by tanks and artillery.

We had no military presence in the area except for a few local militiamen and police-men. I spent the whole of that same day demanding that the Eritrean authorities with-draw their mechanized brigades led by generals. The whole thing was meant to bring us to our knees at gunpoint. On Wednesday, 13 May the Council of Ministers dis-cussed the crisis and issued a positive statement which was approved by parliament. After the Council's statement was transmitted through the media, President Isaais called at about 10 pm. I tried to explain to him the consequences of occupying Ethiopian territory by force. I told him the solution to the crisis was to uncondition-ally withdraw his troops as it was clearly stated in the decision passed by the Council of Ministers.

In subsequent statements the Ethiopian authorities maintained that the Eritrean action was part of a pattern:

[T]he aggression against Ethiopia was, after all, consistent with the Eritrea regime's practice of applying force to promote its interests in the domain of interstate relations. What the Eritrean authorities had done to Yemen, Djibouti and even to Sudan, long before their aggression against Ethiopia, came to mind as a reminder of the clear and dangerous pattern of behaviour that they had been demonstrating with such action in their disdain for international law and/or international organizations.[31]

These views were elaborated and itemized in a 25-point *aide-mémoire* sent by Prime Minister Meles to the Heads of State before the OAU summit in Ouaga-dougou on 17–18 December and summarized in his own statement to the summit, in which he makes it clear that Ethiopia feels that it was Eritrea's aggression which transformed a 'normal border dispute that was being resolved peacefully on the basis of the inviolability of the colonial boundaries into something different'. He also stressed Ethiopia's acceptance of the principles that:

[31] Ethiopian Foreign Ministry statement, 15 December 1998.

1. colonial borders are sacrosanct;
2. border disputes cannot and must not be resolved by force;
3. if and when a country resorts to the use of force, a peaceful resolution of the problem must start by undoing the result of that aggression and by ensuring a return to the *status quo ante*.

6 THE CONFLICT AND ITS AFTERMATH

The first round of fighting

The initial clashes that took place between 6 and 12 May 1998 left the area around Badme badly damaged. Ethiopia claims that the Eritrean action displaced over 24,000 people and destroyed twelve schools, a veterinary clinic, fertilizers and grain stores. After a brief lull the military confrontation between the two countries escalated, with both sides issuing threats of a wider conflict. Ethiopian Foreign Minister Seyoum Mesfin warned that 'all-out war' was possible unless Eritrea withdrew from the territory it had seized, and he declared: 'Ethiopia's patience has its limits.'[32] The troop build-up along the border gained pace rapidly, with reports of up to 200,000 soldiers being deployed. There were patriotic appeals from Addis Ababa to the farmers in Tigray, who were called upon to provide the Ethiopian army with food.

In the event the first round of fighting was brief, bloody, but confined to clashes along the border between 22 May and 11 June. There was also a series of air raids that resulted in a number of civilian casualties. On the ground the fighting centred on three areas: around Sheraro and Badme in the west, around the town of Zalambessa on the road linking the two countries in the centre, and in the far south for control of the road to the Eritrean port of Assab.

The first indication of the scale of the fighting came when Eritrean radio reported Ethiopian attacks on 22, 23 and 25 May on Setit and on 31 May around Aigen and Alitiena. Ethiopian reports confirmed that heavy fighting took place from Sunday, 31 May, around Alitiena. Ethiopia said that the battle was taking place about 20 kilometres inside Ethiopia, and continued until Wednesday, 3 June.

On Tuesday, 2 June, heavy fighting began around the key border town of Zalambessa, for control of the strategically important road linking the two countries. The fighting that began at dawn continued well into Wednesday night, with shells and mortar bombs going off constantly. Thousands of civilians fled the battle, and on Saturday, 6 June, Ethiopia claimed to have retaken the town, but this turned out to be untrue. A Reuters journalist based in Eritrea, touring the town on the following

[32] *Al-Sharq al Awsat*, London, 3 June 1998.

Monday, confirmed that it was still in Eritrean hands. He saw two T-55 and three T-54 tanks in positions around the town and anti-aircraft batteries manned by Eritrean gunners, while Eritrean soldiers were driving around the town in Ethiopian jeeps. Meanwhile other journalists in the town of Adigrat, 25 kilometres south of Zalambessa, reported a mass mobilization of former TPLF guerrilla fighters, and supplies being ferried to the front.

Tuesday, 9 June saw further heavy clashes around Zalambessa, with each side claiming that the other had launched a pre-dawn ground attack. Correspondents on both sides of the border reported intense shelling, mortar and tank fire and saw casualties being taken to hospitals. An Ethiopian commander, Colonel Kiros Fetiwi, said that Eritreans had suffered 'tremendous losses' of men and equipment in repeated attempts to push south from Zalambessa. 'The biggest part of the battle was small arms, hand-to-hand fighting.' He said that the Eritreans attacked at dawn and tried four times during the day to push into Ethiopian-held territory, but were driven back each time.[33]

The fighting around Zalambessa continued on Wednesday the 10th, while thousands of Ethiopians displaced by the fighting were left wandering aimlessly around the town of Adigrat. At least 16,000 men, women and children had fled from the front line. One of them, Shewainesh Meles, said: 'I came here in only what I am wearing. All my clothes and possessions are there. Before this we were like brothers.' Another said: 'Almost half of us were Eritreans ... we were living together and eating together. We will not take revenge on them, but our husbands are fighting against them and they have made us displaced.'[34]

By now the lines around Zalambessa appeared to have stabilized. Eritrea managed to take the town and hold it against repeated Ethiopian counterattacks. For their part the Ethiopians were left holding the road south of the town in strength, preventing an Eritrean advance, but were unable to move forward themselves. In this position the two sides kept a wary eye on each other, with only occasional shelling interrupting the peace as the rainy season made further large-scale offensives difficult to mount.

The conflict was not, however, contained to the ground. On Friday, 5 June, at around 2 pm local time, two Ethiopian MiG-23 jet aircraft attacked the airport at Asmara with rocket and cannon fire. One hour later a second wave of two MiGs attacked the airport again. One person was killed on the ground and five others injured, while a Zambian cargo aircraft was slightly damaged.

The Eritrean air force was also in action, hitting targets in the regional capital, Mekele. A number of civilian targets including a school were hit, and forty-seven

---

[33] Reuters, 9 June 1998.
[34] Reuters, 10 June 1998.

28

people, including ten children, were killed. At least 153 were injured. One Eritrean plane was shot down and its pilot captured. Ethiopia claimed that its raid on Asmara was in retaliation for the attack on Mekele, a charge vehemently denied by Eritrean Air Force Commander Habtezion Hadgu, who said that Ethiopia had bombed Asmara airport first. 'This is tit for tat – one to 100, that's the exchange rate. They hit us, I hit them harder.' Eritrean-based Western diplomats confirmed the commander's version of events, saying the airport attack occurred shortly after 2 pm local time (11 GMT) on Friday and, fifty minutes later, two Eritrean warplanes took off and headed south.[35]

Whoever launched this air war, the Eritreans were clearly embarrassed by the civilian deaths in Mekele. President Afeworki insisted that the fatalities were not deliberate. 'In a war there are flaws here and there and if an aircraft is bombing, it could miss a target and civilians get killed'. Later the president, in a rare public apology, expressed regrets at the deaths, while still insisting that military targets had also been hit.[36] Privately, Eritreans blamed the deaths on the inexperience of their pilots. Either way, the air raids and the civilian deaths led to increasing bitterness, as well as the cancellation of commercial flights into Eritrea.

On Saturday, 6 June, the Ethiopians returned to the air, again attacking Asmara airport at 9.45 am, causing light damage. One aircraft was shot down and its pilot captured. The raid prompted a flurry of diplomatic activity, and both sides agreed to suspend air raids for thirteen hours from 5 pm local time to allow the evacuation of foreign nationals, some 2,000 of whom were stranded in Eritrea. American, Italian, German and British planes hurriedly evacuated their nationals during the temporary halt. The city was reported to be tense, with Eritreans watching the sky nervously, in case the Ethiopian jets returned. The authorities decided that children should be kept at home until Thursday, as a precaution against further raids.

On 11 June two Eritrean helicopters, later joined by a jet fighter, attacked the town of Adigrat at 5.30 pm. Witnesses said the aircraft targeted a bus station, a pharmaceutical factory and a warehouse containing relief food supplies. Four people were killed and around forty injured. Eritrea claimed that the targets were military and that the town was a rear base for Ethiopian military operations on the Zalambessa front.

The fighting on other fronts was more intermittent, less well reported and not witnessed by independent observers. The confrontation reached the area just south of the port of Assab on Friday, 5 June. Troops massed near Mount Mussa Ali engaged in skirmishes, with shelling but apparently no direct confrontation. On Monday, 8 June, the Ethiopian army ordered the evacuation of Bure, a border town

[35] Associated Press, 9 June 1998.
[36] Reuters, 15 June 1998.

80 kilometres southwest of Assab, on the main road linking Addis Ababa with the port of Assab. According to a Western diplomat, the two sides now faced each other across a 6-kilometre stretch of no man's land.[37]

Meanwhile, the Ethiopian government reported further clashes to the west, around Sheraro and Badme. 'The Eritrean army is trying to open several combat fronts in order to scatter the Ethiopian forces,' said a military expert in Addis Ababa. Aid agency sources also reported a heavy build-up of Ethiopian troops around the Humera region, close to the Sudanese border.[38]

On Sunday, 7 June, 57 Eritrean diplomats and their families arrived in Cairo, having being expelled from Addis Ababa. Some complained of not even being allowed to pack their bags. This expulsion marked a further escalation, for it meant that discussions to end the conflict would now have to take place via third parties. Considerable diplomatic efforts were by now under way to end the fighting (see the section below for details) but one intervention bore fruit. President Clinton, speaking to both President Afeworki and Prime Minister Zenawi from Air Force One, managed to secure an end to the air raids. The 'air cease-fire' announced on Sunday, 15 June, was welcomed by Eritrea as a first step towards ending the un-declared war, but Ethiopia issued a communiqué warning: 'We have agreed to an air cease-fire, but if our sovereignty is put under threat we will defend it.'[39]

There were no further reports of clashes on the ground either. Indeed, from Thursday, 11 June, an uneasy cease-fire appeared to be holding. The onset of the rainy season had put an end to the fighting, and apart from some shelling no further major attacks took place. This did not, however, mean that either side stopped its preparations for war, with Ethiopian troop build-ups being reported around the town of Adigrat, while the Eritreans strengthened their hold on Zalambessa. Ethiopian Foreign Minister Seyoum Mesfin said: 'I cannot rule out an all-out war if Eritrea maintains its present intransigent attitude, but we will not rush to war.'[40]

As it became clear that the position had stabilized, civilians began to drift back to the towns they had vacated. Even Zalambessa, the scene of the heaviest confronta-tions, appeared to be coming back to normal, though now under Eritrean, rather than Ethiopian, control. About half of its 20,000 residents had returned by the end of September. Traders had begun opening shops and roadside stalls, and the Saturday market was thriving. A shopkeeper, Kidane Girmay, said that when the fighting erupted he sent his eight children to Addis Ababa, and for him the situation was still not peaceful. 'When I am in my house, I am afraid of the shelling,' he said. 'We expect the war to start every day. But when I am in my shop I am fine because

[37] Agence France Presse (AFP), 9 June 1998.
[38] AFP, 10 June 1998.
[39] Reuters, 15 June 1998.
[40] Associated Press, 15 June 1998.

people come in and we talk. But I am always worried whether I will die today or tomorrow.'[41] Although the town was held by the Eritreans, their officials said that it would be returned to Ethiopia once a peace agreement was achieved.

In October there was a flare-up of artillery activity. On 24 October Ethiopia shelled Zalambessa, while Eritrean guns hit the Ethiopian-held town of Adigrat. The town itself had become heavily garrisoned. Convoys were reported taking troops to and from the front line, which was out of bounds to visiting journalists. The population of 35,000 had doubled with an influx of people fleeing from Zalambessa. Some administrative offices and buildings dug their own bunkers, while residents hollowed out ground shelters to provide some protection in case the city came under shell fire again. 'The problem is not supplies but fear,' said one student. But despite this men, women and children poured onto the streets at night, where markets continue until 8.30 pm.[42]

The changing military balance

There followed several months of uneasy calm. Both sides used this time to continue to purchase arms and ammunition, particularly modern aircraft, and to build up their troop levels. For two countries that have consistently emphasized the need for a peaceful solution to their difficulties, both Ethiopia and Eritrea have been surprisingly prepared to spend, and to spend heavily, on armaments before and after the conflict erupted.

In December 1998 both began to take delivery of significantly improved air capacity. The first of six MiG 29s (Fulcrum) arrived in Asmara. For its part, Ethiopia acquired eight Sukhoi 27s (Flanker), together with a number of Mi 24 (helicopter gunships) and M8 (cargo helicopters). All of these have been obtained from Russia, and according to Russian sources both countries have paid for the deals with cash.

Eritrea has been raising funds from Eritrean communities overseas which have been called on to increase their remittances and their donations to the government war effort. In December Asmara began the sale of treasury bonds to raise further finance for the war. In the last eight months of 1998, Eritrea's defence spending was at least five times its total 1997–8 military budget of under US$100 million. Earlier this year Ethiopia had signed an upgrading deal for its stocks of MiG 21s (thirty) and MiG 23s (twenty) with the Israeli company, Elbit. It also signed a supplementary deal to acquire ten MiG 21s, already upgraded by Elbit for the Romanian air force. However, all this was put on ice following complaints by Eritrea to Israel, and the deal, delayed for a year, is also dependent upon an Ethiopian–Eritrean peace pact.

[41] Associated Press, 28 September 1998.
[42] AFP, 24 November 1998.

Intriguingly, Eritrea originally had no pilots trained to fly MiG 29s, and Ethiopia has none for its Sukhoi 27s, though it did send some to be trained for the upgraded MiG 21s in Romania. The planes which began to arrive in December were accompanied in both cases by a full complement of Russian and east European (Ukrainian) pilots and technicians, twenty in Eritrea and as many in Ethiopia. This fact has been acknowledged by Ethiopian Prime Minister Meles Zenawi, who told the French news agency: 'We have foreign technicians to train our pilots. I assume the Eritreans have foreign technicians.'[43]

Ethiopia gave Eritrea four Mi 17 attack helicopters and loaned it air defence units at the time of the Eritrean conflict with Yemen in 1995. The air defence units were never returned and have proved very useful at Asmara airport where one of Ethiopia's MiG 23s was shot down in June 1998. By August 1999 the Eritrean air force appeared to have lost four of its Mig 29s and had one badly damaged. Ethiopia lost one of its Sukhoi 27s, which crashed at the beginning of December, killing its Russian pilot. The other Sukhois have been largely confined to operations on the Ethiopian side of the border. However, Eritrea claimed to have shot down four Mig 23s and a helicopter in June 1999. If true, this suggests that Asmara has acquired surface-to-air missiles, possibly from Libya.

Ethiopia has acquired tanks (mainly T55s or the equivalent) from China and Bulgaria, though the original China deal was completed before the present crisis blew up. Numbers are still unclear, but some Ethiopian sources claim the deal with Bulgaria was for 210 T55s.

Both sides have also been buying extensive quantities of ammunition. Although both inherited huge stocks of ammunition and supplies from the previous regime, including, for example, the cluster bombs used by Eritrea at Mekele, a good deal of this has now deteriorated beyond use. Ethiopia has been buying from China and eastern Europe, Eritrea from Bulgaria (including a US$50 million deal in June, flown in on Ukrainian transport planes) and Romania; Libya has been one source of finance for these. In all cases, it appears that the suppliers are demanding, and getting, cash up front.

The second round commences

After the first round of fighting ended in June 1998 both countries observed an undeclared truce for the rest of the year, but this did not prevent them from intermittent shelling of each other's positions. On 5 November, the town of Humera close to the Sudanese–Eritrean border was shelled by Eritrean troops. The town's population and the surrounding area – an estimated 30,000 people – were evacuated

[43] AFP, 2 February 1999.

32

to locations 50–60 kilometres from the border. On 17 December three Eritreans were killed during Ethiopian shelling of Tsorona, 85 kilometres south of Asmara. Among the wounded were civilians and soldiers, according to hospital staff.

As peace initiatives came and went the situation on the border became increasingly tense. In January 1999 the Ethiopian ambassador to Kenya said, 'We have restrained ourselves so far, but I don't know how long we can restrain ourselves.' Then in February Ethiopian Prime Minister Meles Zenawi warned that fighting could resume. Along the border, he said, there was a 'very high level of tension that can get out of hand easily and at any time'. Ethiopia closed schools and colleges all along the border, and restricted the movement of foreigners in the area. For its part the Eritrean government declared that it had received a number of reports, including some from Western intelligence sources, that Ethiopia was planning a three-pronged attack between mid-January and mid-February.

The international community also sounded the alarm. On 26 January the Italian Foreign Under-Secretary, Rino Serri, warned that the border war could reignite at any time: 'There is now a high possibility that the war will explode again in a big way.' The following day UN Secretary General Kofi Annan declared that he was 'very, very concerned' about the simmering conflict, and dispatched his special representative, Mohammed Sahnoun, to the region to try to avert a further conflict. There were strenuous and repeated calls for restraint from the UN, European Union, OAU and many states; all to no avail.

At dawn on Saturday, 6 February, the eight-month lull was abruptly brought to an end. Heavy fighting broke out on the Badme front. Ground forces, backed by artillery, were locked in a fierce confrontation, as Ethiopian troops attempted to take Eritrean positions. Each side accused the other of renewing the conflict. Over the next five days a series of clashes took place around Badme and Tsorona. Ethiopian army units, backed by fighter planes and helicopter gunships, pounded Eritrean troop positions. No journalists were allowed on the Ethiopian side of the lines, but those on the Eritrean side reported the Eritreans holding their ground and apparently in good spirits. By Thursday, 10 February, a lull in the fighting had taken place, allowing further diplomatic activity.

The UN Security Council called for an immediate cease-fire and strongly urged all states not to sell arms to either country – somewhat belatedly, given the massive rearmament that had taken place in the previous months. But neither belligerent appeared willing to consider an end to hostilities. 'The Security Council should point the finger at the culprits,' Eritrean presidential spokesman Yemane Gebremeskel said. 'The Ethiopians initiated hostilities when we were both asked to show restraint.' Ethiopia's response was equally uncompromising. 'This call would be better directed at Eritrea,' said Salome Tadesse, Ethiopian government spokeswoman. 'We have been invaded and stayed put for nine months. They cannot ask us not to defend our sovereignty.'

With the fighting apparently stalemated on the Badme front, attention switched to the area around Bure, close to the Eritrean port of Assab. Ethiopia used its air force to attack Eritrean positions and other targets, including the airport north of Assab. No ground troops were apparently deployed and the damage was light.

Towards the end of February there was yet more diplomatic activity. The United States issued a statement saying it deeply regretted Ethiopian use of air power in the conflict, a comment that was rejected by Addis Ababa as 'out of sync with reality'. The European Union attempted to intervene, with German Deputy Foreign Minister Ludger Volmer leading a troika ministerial mission. But the troika's activities were to bear as little fruit as previous diplomatic efforts, and after meeting OAU, Ethiopian and Eritrean officials its members admitted they were unable to persuade the parties to accept a cease-fire. The OAU also attempted to send a mediation committee to Asmara comprising the ambassadors of Burkina Faso, Djibouti and Zimbabwe. The mission never left Addis Ababa. First Eritrea objected to the Djibouti emissary's presence on the team, and then fighting erupted again on the Badme front.

On 23 February Ethiopia launched its most intensive assault on Eritrean positions. Ethiopian troops, supported by heavy artillery, tanks, helicopter gunships and aircraft, attacked Eritrean trenches along a 60-kilometre front. 'Operation Sunset', as the Ethiopians named the offensive, came after Western journalists had reported a 'seemingly endless river of thousands of troops' being brought to the Badme front from Tsorona. For three days the only news put out by Asmara and Addis Ababa was that fighting was intense. Then, on the 26th, Eritrea acknowledged that Ethiopia's 'human wave' attacks had breached its defences. Although declaring that the Ethiopians had suffered heavy losses, the Eritrean statement acknowledged that Ethiopia had broken through, and that Eritrean forces had withdrawn about 20 kilometres to a new front line, leaving the town of Badme in Ethiopian hands.

The next day, 27 February, Eritrean President Isaais Afeworki wrote to the UN Security Council, formally accepting the OAU peace framework.[44] After informal consultations the Security Council issued a statement welcoming Eritrea's acceptance of the OAU plan and calling for an immediate halt to all hostilities so that the agreement could be implemented without delay.

The following day Ethiopia declared that 'a total victory for Ethiopian Defence Forces was achieved on Friday 26 February 1999 in the military counter-offensive named Operation Sunset', adding that Eritrea had suffered a monumental and humiliating defeat, with thousands of casualties and prisoners. Ethiopians went wild with jubilation, celebrating a victory that came close to the anniversary of the battle of Adua, 103 years earlier. Just how extensive the victory actually was is difficult to ascertain, since Addis Ababa did not grant journalists access to the scene of the

[44] The timing was coincidental, according to the Eritrean government.

34

battle, but Western diplomats confirmed that Eritrean forces had suffered a major defeat, with heavy casualties.

Eritrea said it was waiting for a response from Addis Ababa regarding the UN Security Council's call for an immediate cease-fire. While little further fighting took place, Ethiopia remained sceptical of Eritrean intentions, and refused to accept that Asmara had by now complied with the OAU proposal to withdraw from the area around Badme. In a statement on 6 March, Ethiopia accused the Eritreans of attempting only to buy time to reorganize their forces. 'They continue to occupy the Zalambessa-Aiga region, the Bada-Bure region and the Egala region [near Tsorona] … the Eritrean government has shown no signs of withdrawing its army from these territories, as it is required to do by the OAU', the statement said, adding that these areas should be liberated.

The lull turned out to be only another pause in the conflict. The next blow fell at Tsorona, with Eritrea reporting a heavy aerial and artillery bombardment on 13 March, followed by a large-scale ground offensive the following day. This time it was Eritrea that emerged victorious, describing the attack on its well-defended positions as having produced an Ethiopian 'slaughter'. The Eritreans took Western journalists to the scene of the fighting, and they described a narrow front littered with Ethiopian dead. Up to twenty Ethiopian tanks were seen destroyed in an area the size of a football field. Despite the carnage, which may have by now have cost as many as 50,000 lives, the conflict has merited few column inches in the international press. 'The worst war in the world is going on here, but the attention is on Kosovo', an Eritrean fighter complained.[45]

There was no reported ground fighting in April, but in the middle of the month Ethiopian fighter jets bombed the national service training camp at Sawa in south-western Eritrea. In mid-May, Ethiopia again bombed several locations, including the port of Massawa. Heavy battles then took place on the Mereb/Badme front in late May and on several occasions throughout June as Eritrea made two major efforts to retake Badme. Renewed fighting had been widely anticipated as the two sides attempted to secure strategic positions before the rainy season enforced a three-month lull. Neither side made major advances, however.

During the engagements, Ethiopia bombed around Bure and at Assab airport. In mid-June, Eritrea claimed to have downed four Migs and an MI35 helicopter gun-ship which fell 'behind Ethiopian lines'. The Ethiopian spokesperson's office dismissed these claims, saying they had been made 'to ease the concern and pressure felt by the Eritrean soldiers' because 'the aircraft have caused the Eritrean army human and material losses'.[46]

[45] Associated Press, 1 April 1999.
[46] Ethiopian Spokesperson's Office, 16 June 1999.

Ethiopia reported that during these latest battles more than 32,000 Eritrean troops had been killed, wounded or captured. A contemptuous Eritrean communiqué suggested that if these claims – and others that 40,000 Eritreans had been neutralized in earlier actions – were true, the country would be unable to hold its present positions. Eritrea added to its own claims by reporting, in turn, that it had put around 20,000 Ethiopians out of action during the month.

Ethiopia and Eritrea organized visits by journalists to their front lines towards the end of the month. The journalists reported signs of heavy combat, including hand-to-hand fighting from trenches at points no more than 50 metres apart. However, the visits on both sides were carefully stage-managed and neither side's wider claims could be verified.

7 THE CONFLICT SPREADS OUTWARDS

When President Clinton toured Africa in March and April 1998, praising young and dynamic leaders for being the standard-bearers of an 'African renaissance', President Afeworki and Prime Minister Meles Zenawi were precisely the kind of politicians he had in mind. Hardworking, uncorrupt and determined to break with the continent's sleazy and violent past, both men were promoted as role models, carving a new destiny for Africa. Their governments were seen as running just the kind of self-reliant regimes that international agencies such as the World Bank and International Monetary Fund could cooperate with. All in all, they represented the way ahead for the entire region. The conflict has left that image in tatters, and has critically affected international relations both within and beyond the Horn of Africa.

It not only shattered American confidence that it had found regional actors upon whom it could rely, it also had dramatic consequences for every country in the region. All have found themselves drawn into the escalating war. Djibouti, for example, has discovered that its attempts to act as an honest broker between its neighbours have been rebuffed, and it has been forced to take sides. Somalia has found that its internal disputes have been exacerbated as Ethiopia and Eritrea strengthen their Somali allies to further their own war aims. But perhaps the most startling development has been the transformation of the status of Sudan from regional pariah to major regional actor, wooed by both Asmara and Addis Ababa.

Sudan

Prior to the conflict the United States had seen both Eritrea and Ethiopia as vital to its policy of building a bulwark against the spread of Islamic fundamentalism of the kind promoted by the Sudanese government. Both countries supported these American goals for their own ends. Ethiopia had for many years provided a safe haven for the rebel Sudan People's Liberation Army of John Garang, which has been resisting the extension of Islamic and Arab control over southern Sudan. Eritrea also fell out with the authorities in Khartoum, blaming them for backing Islamic movements fighting against the EPLF, and responded by supporting and providing a sanctuary for movements hostile to the Sudanese government. But after May 1998 it became clear to both Ethiopia and Eritrea that they could not afford a hostile neighbour to their west. First Addis Ababa and then Asmara set about trying to rebuild relations with Khartoum, much to the chagrin of the Americans.

Arab states have taken a leading role in trying to mediate between Sudan and Eritrea. Libya and Qatar have been responsible for a number of discussions and meetings, which finally led to an agreement between President Omar el-Bashir and President Isaais Afeworki, signed in Doha on 2 May 1999. Qatar has had close relations with Eritrea since it became independent. In a deal financed by Saudi Arabia, it provided tanks and armoured personnel carriers in October 1995, following Eritrea's break with Sudan. In October 1998, the Qatari Foreign Minister Hamad ibn Jassem al-Thani visited Asmara and Khartoum in an attempt to bring both countries to the negotiating table.

In early November 1998 Sudan and Eritrea accepted a Qatari invitation to talks. On 10 November, after forty-eight hours of discussions, the foreign ministers of Sudan and Eritrea signed a memorandum of understanding about how future talks would resolve differences between their two countries. The memorandum was reported to have provided for the two countries 'to respect their respective political choices and not to interfere in each other's internal affairs'.[47]

This did not appear to have much effect until a meeting at the Libyan-sponsored Committee of Sahel-Saharan States (Comessa), which Eritrea joined in April. The Sudanese and Eritrean presidents, under heavy Libyan pressure, agreed to meet in Doha. The six-point agreement provides for the two countries to restore diplomatic relations, respect each other's political choices, refrain from supporting each other's opponents, work to resolve differences and establish a joint committee to examine remaining issues, especially those relating to security.[48]

President Bashir called the agreement an 'advanced step' towards normalizing relations and ending disputes; President Afeworki said Eritrea was 'completely convinced of the need to go beyond mistakes made in the past, and circumstances now favour a normalization'. Despite their support for each other's opposition, both countries had pressing reasons for trying to improve relations by March 1999. Eritrea, following its defeat at Badme in February, was anxious to limit its exposure to a war on two fronts and was concerned by the unification of the Eritrean opposition. Sudan was concerned over the security of the pipeline from the el-Obeid oil field to Port Sudan, due to start operations at the end of June.

[47] AFP, 10 November 1998.
[48] Sudan TV, 2 May 1999.

The agreement was another blow to the Sudanese opposition umbrella movement, the National Democratic Alliance (NDA), which had its headquarters in the former Sudanese embassy in Asmara. It had been deeply worried by the deterioration in the relations of its main backers, Ethiopia and Eritrea, over the previous year. Soon after the Ethio-Eritrean conflict erupted, Ethiopia began talks with the government in Khartoum. Commercial flights were restored, and the offices of the Sudan People's Liberation Front of John Garang, which had long relied on Ethiopian support for its operations in eastern Sudan, were closed. In September, Sadiq al-Mahdi of the Umma Party, one of the main constituents of the NDA, went to Addis Ababa and then Asmara in an attempt to mediate between the two capitals. Although he said he saw a 'ray of hope', nothing came of his efforts.[49]

The NDA held a conference in Eritrea between 28 September and 3 October 1998. Its final communiqué, broadcast over its own radio station, talked of preparations for the overthrow of the Sudanese government and expressed profuse thanks to President Afeworki for the 'openness and participatory spirit' he had displayed during the meeting which 'reflected Eritrea's firm determination to continue in solidarity and support with the Sudanese people'.[50]

Sudan continued to accuse Eritrea, along with Uganda, of providing military support to the NDA. In September, the Sudanese authorities declared a general mobilization to confront what it said was an attack by Uganda and Eritrea in the south of the country. In an interview with Reuters, Sudanese Foreign Minister Mustafa Osman Ismail said that Uganda had over 2,000 troops inside southern Sudan, supported by Eritrean tank crews. He also confirmed that Sudan for its part was backing rebel movements fighting against the governments in both Uganda and Eritrea. Eritrea had complained of cross-border raids from Sudan by the Eritrean Liberation Front of Abdullah Idris and Eritrean Islamic Jihad rebels since 1993. Asked about support for Ugandan and Eritrean rebels, the Sudanese Foreign Minister replied: 'Why should we hide it? It is a fact.'[51]

Eritrea has taken a less open view; while consistently promising to use all possible means to overthrow the government in Khartoum, it has persistently denied any direct military involvement. When the Agence France Presse correspondent in Asmara, Ruth Simon, reported that President Afeworki had told a meeting of the ruling Popular Front for Democracy and Justice (PFDJ) – at which she, as a party member, was present – that Eritrean troops had suffered casualties in Sudan, she was promptly arrested and detained for eighteen months. She was only released in December 1998, without having been charged or tried.

[49] *Al Hayat*, 16 September 1998.
[50] BBC Monitoring Service, 5 October 1998.
[51] Reuters, 23 October 1998.

It remains to be seen what effect the May 1999 agreement will have on the NDA. In December, President Afeworki told the NDA, after the meeting of Sudanese and Eritrean foreign ministers in Doha, that Eritrean links with the Sudanese opposition were long-standing, having come about before the current regime took power in Khartoum, and that they would not be broken.[52] A few days later, the Eritrean Foreign Minister, Haile Wolde Tensai, on a visit to Khartoum, insisted that Eritrea wanted more than a condemnation of terrorism, it needed 'actions and not just statements'.[53] Eritrea had less room for manoeuvre by May 1999, and the NDA are certainly more alarmed; before the ink was dry on the agreement, the NDA launched an attack on a military barracks in the Kassala district, as part of an effort to cut the Port Sudan–Khartoum road.

Any NDA attempt to undermine the agreement will also be welcomed by the Eritrean opposition alliance, the Alliance of Eritrean National Forces (AENF), created on 6 March 1999, and based in Khartoum. This brought together ten Eritrean opposition groups, largely Muslim, but including several Ethiopian-backed Marxist groups, and most of the former ELF fragments.[54] One other Ethiopian-based movement, the Afar Red Sea Democratic Front, organized in 1998, has not joined the AENF, which otherwise represents most of the opponents of the PFDJ. The AENF represents groups that draw most support from the Muslim population of Eritrea, though the ELF Revolutionary Council does still have Christian support. Though derided by the Eritrean government, the umbrella organization does include at least three movements which have some military experience and can probably put some 3,000 fighters into the field.

The AENF is as worried as the Sudanese opposition, the NDA, about any Sudanese–Eritrean rapprochement. It has reportedly been assured by President Bashir that the agreement will not affect its status, though this has not been clarified. Only a week after his meeting with President Afeworki in May 1999, President Bashir took the opportunity to hold talks with Ethiopian Prime Minister Meles Zenawi during the inauguration of Djibouti's new president. Observers said they agreed on numerous issues in discussions which apparently covered Eritrean–Sudanese relations and the Ethiopian–Eritrean conflict.[55] The AENF does, however, have one significant advantage over the NDA. If Sudan is closed to it, it could move its base to Ethiopia; the NDA has no such option.

[52] BBC Monitoring Service, 6 December 1998.
[53] *Al-Zaman*, 16 December 1998.
[54] See Appendix 5 for a list of groups making up the organization.
[55] Republic of Sudan Radio, 9 May 1999.

40

Exporting conflict

Ethiopia's and Sudan's efforts to increase opposition to the government in Asmara have been paralleled by extensive Eritrean efforts to build up resistance to the authorities in Addis Ababa. Asmara is now actively attempting to restrict Ethiopia's use of the port of Djibouti, is supporting opposition groups involved in armed struggle in southern Ethiopia, including the Oromo Liberation Front (OLF), the Ogaden National Liberation Front and al-Itahaad al-Islami, and is disrupting Ethiopia's network of alliances in Somalia.

Djibouti has gained significance from the diversion of Ethiopian imports and exports after Ethiopian links through Eritrea were cut. But these gains have not been without some cost. The fighting that took place on the border south of the Eritrean port of Assab was dangerously close to the frontier with Djibouti; and Eritrea complained that Djibouti was aiding the Ethiopian war effort. These protests were underlined when Eritrea sent a delegation to Djibouti, led by Foreign Minister Haile Wolde Tensai on 10 September 1998.

At the time President Hassan Gouled Aptidon of Djibouti was attempting to mediate between his two warring neighbours, but Eritrea requested that Djibouti drop out of the OAU's High Level Committee that met in Ouagadougou on 7 and 8 November 1998, accusing it of collaborating with the Ethiopian war effort. Djibouti was furious, accusing Eritrea of making baseless accusations, and President Afeworki of insulting President Hassan Gouled. On 18 November it severed diplomatic relations with Asmara and expelled the Eritrean ambassador.

More serious was Eritrea's backing for the Djibouti opposition Front pour la Restauration de l'Unité et la Démocratie (FRUD) of former Prime Minister Ahmed Dini, allowing it a base in southern Eritrea and providing arms. The first result of this came in October, with a FRUD attack on an Ethiopian road convoy near the border *en route* from Djibouti to Addis Ababa. Following this Ethiopian troops moved in to help the Djibouti government with security along the road and rail links, and in the largely Afar areas. Most of the support for FRUD comes from the Afar, and its units operate largely in northern Djibouti, close to the Eritrean-occupied Mount Mussa Ali, where the borders of all three countries meet. Ethiopian troops and helicopters were in action at least twice in the first months of 1999, but land mine explosions on at least four occasions prior to the presidential elections of April demonstrated FRUD's ability to continue its activities. Djibouti's new president, Ismail Omar Guelleh, was elected in April. Born and educated in Ethiopia, he is unlikely to change the present close relationship, and indeed has spoken of the need for even closer links with Djibouti's larger neighbour.

As part of its attempt to woo the Afars who live in Ethiopia, Eritrea has also been making overtures to the divided Afar Liberation Front of Sultan Alimirreh. The leader of one faction, Habib Alimirreh, one of the Sultan's sons, went to Asmara in late 1998. The leader of another ALF faction, Hanfare, the Sultan's eldest son, returned to Ethiopia from exile in Saudi Arabia early in 1999. Ethiopia's creation of the Afar Red Sea Democratic Front in 1998 was, equally, an attempt to organize existing discontent among Eritrea's Afars. Ethiopia has yet to make any serious overtures to the main Afar opposition group in Ethiopia, the Afar Revolutionary Democratic United Front, which supports the creation of a single Afar state, within Ethiopia, for the Afars of both Eritrea and Ethiopia. This is surprising as such a development might allow for more direct Ethiopian control over the port of Assab in the future.

In the later part of 1998, Eritrea also set in motion a more general policy of attempting to organize Ethiopian opposition movements. The government in Asmara has long had links with the Oromo Liberation Front, and attempted to mediate between it and the newly installed government in Addis Ababa when relations between the two broke down in 1992, and the OLF made a largely unsuccessful attempt to launch an armed struggle. In April 1998, the OLF elected a more militant leadership at a congress held in Mogadishu, Somalia, under the protection of one of the Mogadishu 'warlords', Hussein Mohammed Farah 'Aydeed', whose relations with the EPRDF government in Addis Ababa were poor.[56] This is not the place to enter into a discussion of the complexities of Somali politics, but Hussein 'Aydeed' was one of those faction leaders who did not take part in the Ethiopian-sponsored Sodere reconciliation conference in January 1997, but did attend the Egyptian-sponsored Cairo reconciliation conference of October 1997. He has had close links with the OLF and the Oromo National Liberation Front (ONLF), as well as with al-Itahaad. OLF fighters have fought in his militia against the Rahenweyne Resistance Army, in Bay and Bakool regions, and he has provided the OLF with weapons.

In August 1998, Hussein 'Aydeed' visited Addis Ababa and signed a number of agreements. The Ethiopian government believed the visit had solved most of the outstanding problems. But it apparently made the mistake of failing to offer any specific military assistance. Eritrea made no such mistake. Six months later, when Hussein 'Aydeed' visited Asmara, he came away with promises of considerable military aid, and returned to Mogadishu by air with a planeload of arms, reportedly financed by Libya and flown via Yemen. At least two other planeloads were flown in, and subsequently two shiploads of weaponry arrived at the port of Merca, in March and May 1999. Many of these weapons, mostly light arms, but including heavy machine guns and anti-aircraft guns, have gone to the OLF and to the ONLF. Somali sources claim that an Oromo training camp was set up at Qorioli, and that in

---

[56] The name 'Aydeed' is in inverted commas since it is a nickname, and not a given name, but it is the name by which he is best known. This is a common practice among Somalis.

May several hundred more Oromos arrived from Eritrea, where they had been training, together with Eritrean officers, including engineers and mine-laying experts.[57] A third shipload, including another 450 Oromo fighters, arrived in June. Eritrea has denied providing any assistance or arms to the OLF or to anti-Ethiopian Somali factions.

Both the OLF and the ONLF increased their activity significantly in 1998–9. The OLF has been operating in southern Ethiopia along the Kenyan border area, and Ethiopian troops have carried out hot pursuit operations into Kenya on a number of occasions following OLF attacks on military posts. Ethiopia believes the Kenyan authorities have made little effort to clamp down on OLF activity, despite reports in the Kenyan press of groups of 200 or 300 heavily armed fighters basing themselves inside Kenya; Oromos live on both sides of the border. Kenya did reinforce security along its border after eighteen died in an Ethiopian attack in January 1999. It has now asked the United Nations High Commission for Refugees (UNHCR) to move the 108,000 Somali refugees living in three camps in northeastern Kenya back into Somalia.

The ONLF has also increased its activities, carrying out two kidnappings in the first months of 1999. According to its leader, Muhammed Umar Uthman, the Ethiopian government had thwarted all efforts to hold a dialogue, leaving the ONLF with no alternative but to escalate its military activities. Admiral Muhammed, a former head of the Somali navy, said dozens of Ethiopian troops were killed every month, with seventy-eight killed and fifty-nine wounded in February.[58] In March there were reports in Mogadishu that trucks of arms and ammunition were going up to the Ethiopian border, presumably for use by the ONLF or al-Itahaad.

Eritrea is now sponsoring efforts to organize a 'Coalition of Ethiopian Oppressed Peoples', an idea underlined at an OLF meeting in Stockholm on 3 April 1999, which included representatives from various Oromo groups, and from the Sidama Liberation Movement.[59] Eritrea would like to see anti-Ethiopian Somali groups, including the factions of Hussein 'Aydeed' and his allies, also involved in this coalition.

Ethiopia has responded to these efforts to widen the war by continuing its support for anti-Hussein 'Aydeed' factions in Somalia, and for any opposed to al-Itahaad.[60] General 'Morgan', who was based in Kismayo, used his latest consignment to attack al-Itahaad training camps around Ras Kamboni in southwestern Somalia on 14 April 1999, forcing al-Itahaad fighters to take refuge in Kenya.

[57] *Qaran*, Mogadishu, 6 May 1999; AFP, 28 April 1999.
[58] *Al-Hayat*, 29 March 1999.
[59] The groups involved include the OLF, which formed a military alliance with the ONLF in 1996, and has signed agreements with two smaller Oromo organizations, the Oromo People's Liberation Organization (on 14 March), and the United Oromo People's Liberation Front (on 21 March).
[60] See Appendix 6 for a list of those organizations receiving Ethiopian and Eritrean assistance.

Ethiopia has also crossed the Somali border on a number of occasions since 1996 to try to neutralize al-Itahaad and the ONLF – it regards the two organizations as two sides of the same coin. Dolo, Luq and a number of smaller towns were held by Ethiopia for most of 1997. Another Ethiopian incursion took place in early April, to support an opposition faction of the Somali National Front (SNF) in Gedo region. The SNF's leader, General Omar Haji Mohamed, joined Hussein 'Aydeed' in 1998, precipitating a split in the SNF and giving Ethiopia the opportunity for further intervention in the region. On 11 April the Mogadishu allies of General Omar, Hussein 'Aydeed' and Ali Mahdi, formally complained to the UN, copying their complaint to the OAU, the Arab League and the Inter-Governmental Authority for Development. Ethiopian troops returned at the beginning of June, acting in support of their SNF allies, and supporting the Rahenweyne Resistance Army against Hussein 'Aydeed' in the capture of Baidoa in June. There were indications in July that Ethiopia was prepared to increase troop levels significantly to ensure that all Eritrean support for Hussein 'Aydeed' or the OLF was nipped in the bud.

Both Ethiopia and Kenya have been concerned by the continued anarchy in Somalia and the failure of southern Somali factions to produce the sort of clan-based regional administrations that have appeared in the northwest (Somaliland) and northeast (Puntland). Both countries are also alarmed by the ease with which Eritrea appears to have become involved. There are also reports, of concern to the United States, that Osama bin Laden might be thinking of relocating to Somalia from Afghanistan.[61] There is some reason to believe that al-Itahaad had some links with bin Laden in the past. There have been suggestions that bin Laden has training camps in the Bajun Islands, but evidence for this is minimal. Al-Itahaad itself had camps in southern Somalia, near Ras Kamboni, but these were the target of operations by General 'Morgan' from Kismayo in April, and there is nothing to suggest they have ever had the level of expertise or size that would indicate activity by bin Laden. The reports, however, were sufficient to persuade the US ambassador in Nairobi to warn Hussein 'Aydeed' that any continued use of US passports by his wife and family would certainly be dependent upon total non-involvement with bin Laden.

Wider implications of the conflict

The United States has attempted, from the first, to maintain good relations with both sides, but in the process it has managed to anger both Eritrea and Ethiopia. In 1998, it was Eritrea that was affronted by what it saw as a clumsy effort at mediation by the United States, one which, essentially, took Ethiopia's position. It had failed to

---

[61] Osama bin Laden is a wealthy Saudi who has been accused of backing a number of Islamic anti-Western movements, and is considered a terrorist financier by the United States.

show the balance required of a mediator, and President Isaais Afeworki was outspoken in his criticisms, and personally dismissive of the Assistant Secretary of State Susan Rice. He was equally critical of the OAU's endorsement of the US proposals and the UN's backing of them. His comments reinforced his reputation for arrogance and gained Eritrea few friends in either organization.

In recent months Ethiopia has felt that the United States had failed to put the necessary pressure on Eritrea to encourage it to withdraw; it was, subsequently, seriously upset by the US-backed UN call for an arms embargo, which it saw as a failure to acknowledge Ethiopia's position as a victim of aggression; and by Secretary of State Madeleine Albright's call for an unconditional cease-fire along the border.

The United States has therefore been left with its major policy in the Horn, the containment of Sudan, in shreds and with its regional allies at each other's throats. These have been serious reverses, but they have not persuaded Washington to give up on the region. It has continued to attempt to mediate in the dispute, through the work of former National Security Council Adviser Anthony Lake, who has travelled to both capitals in an attempt to resolve the crisis. So far these efforts have failed, like those of all other mediators.

Israel, which has had close relations with both Eritrea and Ethiopia, has managed to preserve links with both, but only just. Its main preoccupation remains, as always, to find a way of keeping Arab control of the Red Sea within bounds, and to keep open an exit through the southern end of the sea at the Bab el Mandeb straits. It was quick to recognize the existence of Eritrea as soon as it acquired *de facto* independence in May 1991, despite the fact that it had been supplying arms to the Ethiopian dictatorship of Mengistu Haile Mariam only three months earlier. Relations have subsequently been close, and when seriously ill with cerebral malaria President Afeworki was treated in Israel. Both countries continue to deny that Israel received facilities in the Dahlak islands in return for Israeli military assistance, though Israel was certainly sympathetic towards Eritrea during its clash with Yemen over the Hanish islands in 1995.

Israel, however, also has long-standing ties with Ethiopia, and an emotional commitment to the still sizeable community of Falasha, or Ethiopian Jews, though the majority of these were moved to Israel in 1984 ('Operation Moses') and 1991 ('Operation Solomon'). Ethiopia remains its second largest trading partner in Africa. The 1998 agreement by an Israeli company to upgrade over fifty of Ethiopia's ageing Russian planes, although postponed after strong representations, irritated Eritrea greatly.

Israel's failure to come out in clear support of Eritrea may have played a part in Asmara's decision 1998 to move towards the Arab world, and in particular towards Libya, with which it now has close links. There were originally indications that Eritrea was trying to use its contacts with Libya as a means of encouraging both the

United States and Israel to be more supportive. However, President Afeworki has made several trips to Tripoli since summer 1998, and Libya has funded a number of Eritrea's arms purchases. Eritrea has made known its interest in becoming a member of the Arab League; and following the 1998 decision of the International Tribunal to award most of the disputed Hanish islands to Yemen, it lost no time in repairing relations with that country. Yemen, however, remains cautious about Eritrea's Red Sea policies. The two states continue to be rivals for resources and for the strategic control of the lower Red Sea.

8 ECONOMIC CONSEQUENCES OF THE CONFLICT

Bilateral trade before and after May 1998

From the end of the war in 1991 until late 1997 bilateral trade between Ethiopia and Eritrea flourished, thanks to the *de facto* currency union and a progressive dismantling of trade barriers between the two. The staple, *teff*, and other grains and foodstuffs were exported from Ethiopia to Eritrea, while Eritrean enterprises gradually re-established export markets, notably in the northern highlands, lost during the decades of war to 1991. Real progress was also made in amicably disentangling the complex relations that had existed prior to Eritrean independence over issues including joint finances, liabilities, pensions and assets. Assab remained the principal conduit for Ethiopia's foreign trade. After a brief, costly experiment with leased airlines, Eritrean exporters successfully used Ethiopian Airlines' unrivalled African and international network to export their manufactured goods.

This arrangement faltered in late 1997. Following the rejection of the dual currency 1:1 parity by Ethiopia's political and monetary authorities, Eritrea's leadership made plain its discontent with the new arrangement. Eritrea's government clearly interpreted Ethiopia's rejection of the dual currency arrangement as an affront. From December 1997 Asmara appears to have dissuaded its merchants from trading with Ethiopia. Although the Commercial Bank of Ethiopia had already established letters of credit to facilitate dollar-denominated bilateral trade, Eritreans shunned such facilities and trade stagnated. With supplies severely restricted, the price of Ethiopian products in Eritrea naturally increased. This compounded the initial, inevitable price confusion surrounding the introduction of the nakfa within Eritrea. Until May, a limited range of Ethiopian goods nevertheless continued to be available in Eritrea. Many apparently arrived quasi-illicitly, particularly via Assab. Price uncertainty surrounding the nakfa also had an impact on remittances from Tigrayans working in Eritrea, and thus had a knock-on effect on the Tigrayan economy.

Ethiopia's distinctly precipitous decision to divert all foreign trade via Djibouti in May 1998 had significant logistical implications as the vast majority of imports and exports arrive and depart by sea. This includes the supply of petroleum products, for which Ethiopia is entirely dependent on imports. The Djibouti port authorities immediately put in place a series of emergency measures to facilitate the increased flow of goods through the port. Despite dire predictions to the contrary, at least until early 1999 Djibouti's port, road and rail links managed with surprising efficiency to handle the upsurge in Ethiopian cargo. Major bottlenecks were avoided, although bulk cargo-handling facilities – notably for import of food aid and fertilizer – were under considerable strain. But this route is precarious. The vast majority is trucked via Galafi, which is within striking distance of the Ethiopian–Eritrean border. If the fighting along the border were to spill over into Djibouti it could sever this link, putting Ethiopian fuel imports and vital coffee exports in jeopardy. Some trade might be diverted through the Somaliland port of Berbera, which has acted as a conduit for transit goods to Ethiopia in recent years, but it could not take up the full scope of Ethiopian trade if Djibouti were no longer available.

Economic impact of the conflict on Ethiopia

Since 1992 Ethiopia has been undertaking a substantial economic reform programme. Reforms have received the backing of major multilateral donors, most conspicuously and significantly the World Bank. During 1998 the Bank announced almost $1 billion of new lending to Ethiopia for the period 1998–2001, and actual disbursements made Ethiopia the tenth largest recipient of Bank lending in 1998. The Ethiopian authorities gained considerable international praise for their reform programme, and in September 1998, in conjunction with the IMF, published a policy framework paper, highlighting a three-year economic programme.[62] Although finalized after the outbreak of the conflict, the document makes virtually no mention of its potential impact upon Ethiopia's reforming economy. Yet the war is likely to influence medium-term reform in three areas.

- Ethiopia is dependent upon continued flows of highly concessional lending and substantial debt relief. Although the government accepts that the current economic impact of the fighting on Tigray and the northeastern Afar region has been substantial, given that 300,000 people have been displaced, it maintains that the overall impact on the economy has been 'very limited'. However, Neway Gebre-Ab, the Prime Minister's chief economic adviser, said that some countries have withheld bilateral assistance, something he termed a 'very unfortunate signal'.[63] A cut in aid flows and debt relief would require a substantial revision of economic plans.

[62] This is available at http://imfn1x.imr.org/external/np/pfp/eth/etp.htm.
[63] Reuters, 12 April 1999.

- Even with no resumption of fighting and a continued stalemate, military expenditure rose sharply in 1998, and the availability of foreign exchange has fallen owing to arms purchases. Current predictions for foreign trade earnings, and revenue from tariffs, assume no disruption of trade links via Djibouti.
- Many structural reforms are likely to be retarded by the conflict. These include civil service reform, financial-sector restructuring and an ambitious privatization programme. Sectoral investment programmes on health, education and road construction are also likely to suffer, either through reduced donor support, or because they depend crucially upon ongoing administrative and regional reforms. Similarly, current projections for domestic and foreign investment are likely to prove over-optimistic in the event of renewed conflict.

Donors remain circumspect and cautious about the likely economic impact of the war. Publicly the IMF simply notes that 'a timely and peaceful resolution of the unsettled border dispute with Eritrea is essential to bolster economic prospects'.

Although Ethiopia has ceased formal trade altogether with Eritrea, the aggregate national effect has not been significant. However, there are two obvious qualifications to this.

First, the suspension of trade represents an unnecessary loss of the most easily accessible neighbouring market. Previously poor relations with Sudan have stunted cross-border trade in the northeast. Eritrea represents a 'natural' market for many Ethiopian goods, particularly agricultural produce grown in northern Ethiopia. Following the good main crop harvests in 1998 grain prices in Ethiopia fell sharply. Though beneficial to food-deficit areas, this nevertheless depressed agricultural incomes overall. The suspension of grain and livestock exports to Eritrea further depressed both grain and livestock prices in Gondar and Tigray. In the longer term an indefinite suspension of trade also negates plans for hydroelectric development in Ethiopia, which has considerable long-term export prospects to both Sudan and Eritrea.

Second, and probably most important for the current crisis, the economic impact of the break in trade with Eritrea has a disproportionate impact on Tigray itself. With its greater concentration of industry and higher living standards, Eritrea has long been a source of employment for Tigrayans. Trade with Eritrea is also proportionally far more important for neighbouring Tigray than it is for other regions in Ethiopia. The introduction of the nakfa and the problems of converting nakfa into birr in its first month of operation created considerable hardship and disruption for Tigrayans hitherto dependent upon employment in, or trade with, Eritrea. Indeed it is possible that the impact of this factor, notably on Axum, influenced how the (largely Tigrayan) Ethiopian leadership initially reacted to the border dispute.

Economic implications for Eritrea and for integration in the Horn

The potential impact of the conflict on Eritrea is far harder to gauge, for a variety of reasons: a weak statistical base, lack of independent indigenous verification or debate on the Eritrean economy, and the tighter, more direct control that the political leadership exerts over the far smaller economy. The short-term impact appears to have been mitigated by increased flows of remittances from Eritreans abroad. Nevertheless, three points emerge.

First, Eritrea's loss of trade with Ethiopia cannot but represent a significant brake on economic activities in Eritrea. Eritrea's trade with Ethiopia, both in terms of exports (mainly manufactures: clothing, shoes, drinks, etc.) and imports (notably coffee and grains), is considerable, generally thought to account for 50 per cent of foreign trade prior to May 1998. However, it should be noted that: (i) the disruption of trade dates from December, i.e. it predates the border dispute; and (ii) it was at Eritrea's instigation that trade was suspended. Whether this was a calculated response, which fits within a longer-term economic strategy, or simply a knee-jerk reaction to Ethiopia's rejection of the idea of a dual currency area, the Eritrean leadership clearly believes it can trade elsewhere.

Second, Eritrea's physical links with the rest of the world have been severely disrupted by the Ethiopian authorities' decision to suspend Ethiopian Airlines flights to and from Asmara. Evidently this prevents travel between Addis Ababa and Asmara. But far more importantly, Ethiopian Airlines was the carrier most used by Eritreans to fly to Europe. Unless the Eritrean authorities are able to rapidly replace these connecting flights, travel to and from Asmara is likely to become difficult for as long as the crisis persists.

Third, the main short-term impact of the switch from Assab (and to a lesser extent the northern port of Massawa) upon Eritrea is simply a loss of invisible earnings in terms of port fees. While not insignificant, these are not essential to government income. Use of Assab is almost entirely for transit to Ethiopia, the city being geographically isolated from the bulk of Eritrea's population. If transit trade is not restored, even in part, then longer-term employment prospects in Assab will be minimal.

However, the authorities in Asmara are acutely sensitive to suggestions that the war may be eroding the economic base. Reports appeared in April 1999 quoting the chief economic adviser to the Finance Ministry, Woldai Futur, as saying that the growth rate had halved in 1998 to 4 per cent, from 8 per cent the previous year. The government reacted by putting out official denials, maintaining that the economy was 'growing well', particularly when compared with the rest of sub-Saharan Africa which managed only 2.4 per cent growth.[64]

---

[64] Reuters, 12 April 1999; Embassy of Eritrea in statement, 'Reuters fumbles again', 20 April 1999.

The long-term setback for economic integration and attempts to boost growth and alleviate poverty in the region as a whole is substantial. In the immediate aftermath of the May 1993 referendum which endorsed Eritrean independence, Isaais Afeworki stated that his long-term goal was federation, and the creation of one economic entity in the Horn of Africa. Many existing links made Ethiopian–Eritrean ties the heart of any such project. The apparently amicable disentangling of two state structures, and the flourishing bilateral trade and investment in the period 1993–8, suggested that such a project might be feasible. The success of the regional forum, the Intergovenmental Agency for Development (IGAD), and infrastructural developments, particularly those supported by multilateral donors including the World Bank and the European Union, depend on good relations between Asmara and Addis. The May 1998 conflict, and the ensuing expulsions and the cutting of trade links, completely undermine this vision.

9 THE HUMAN COST

The conflict has exacted a high human toll. By March 1999, there were reported to be as many as 50,000 military dead, with the numbers of injured and captured understood to be commensurately high.[65] Since then there has been further heavy fighting. One of the curious anomalies has been the disparity between claims of 'some thousands' of prisoners being captured, for example at Badme in February, and the hundreds, at most, that have so far been seen by the Red Cross. The International Committee of the Red Cross (ICRC) has not been granted access to prisoners of war by Asmara, and only to some by Addis Ababa. There have been hundreds of civilian deaths and injuries resulting, for example, from Eritrea's bombing of Mekele and Adigrat in June 1998 and from Ethiopian shelling of border villages in early 1999. While the few hundred civilian casualties seem small compared with the scale of the conflict, the reason becomes clear in the light of the type of war that is being fought. With hostilities confined mainly to trench warfare, civilians have been largely out of the line of fire, and the main collateral damage has been in terms of displacement, as people have either fled or been cleared by troops from combat areas. With a 1,000-km front line, by March 1999 more than 800,000 people in the two countries were reported as having been displaced from villages and towns along or close to the common border.

During the first round of fighting in May and June 1998, Eritrea made military advances into Ethiopian territory and consequently it was Ethiopians who were displaced in the greatest numbers. By the end of the year, official Ethiopian government and UN reports recorded around 400,000 displaced, of whom three-quarters were in Tigray and the remainder in Afar.[66] Initially, the authorities tried to house people with still settled communities rather than in camps which, since the 1985 famine, most Ethiopians have associated with disease and death. As the numbers of displaced escalated, however, it became impossible to avoid camps altogether. By

[65] *The Economist*, 8 May 1999, p. 73. This estimate must be treated with caution, since neither side publishes its own casualties, while exaggerating the losses inflicted on its opponents.
[66] *Emergency Assistance Proposal for War Displaced People in Tigray*, Relief Society of Tigray, January 1999. *Assessment Report*, UN Emergency Unit for Ethiopia, January 1999.

the end of 1998, with peace talks apparently going nowhere, Ethiopia was making contingency plans for renewed fighting and for an anticipated further quarter of a million displaced.

In January 1999, Eritrea's official relief agency was reporting 100,000 Eritreans displaced and 250,000 whose lives had been disrupted by the war but who were not completely destitute. The Eritrean authorities assumed that the situation of 'no-war-no-peace', which had held through the latter half of 1998, would continue and their plans for 1999 made no provision for major increases in the numbers of war-affected civilians. When, in February 1999, Ethiopia pushed back Eritrean troops from the positions that they had held in Badme since June, 100,000 Eritreans were displaced, bringing the total number of people whose lives had been completely or partly disrupted by the conflict to 450,000, or over 10 per cent of the population.[67] As one of the poorest nations in the world, Eritrea has no means to provide for all these people. Reluctantly, the authorities have turned for help to international aid agencies which they had unceremoniously dismissed in 1997, claiming at that time that Eritrea wished to avoid depending on external aid and could manage without them. This takes place at a time when the United Nations and aid agency staff are expressing concern about the drought provoked food crisis, which is already being compared with the 1985 famine.

The large numbers of displaced have put the resources of both countries under severe strain. Added to this group, however, there have been more than 40,000 Ethiopians in Eritrea and more than 50,000 Eritreans in Ethiopia who have crossed the border to return home, voluntarily or as a result of coercion, and who are almost all destitute. These people represent one more bone of contention between the belligerents, adding to their already long catalogue of grievances against each other. Hundreds of thousands of Ethiopian citizens are Eritrean in origin and for decades Eritrea has hosted tens of thousands of Ethiopian migrants, one sign of the interconnectedness of the two economies. Some of the Ethiopians in Eritrea had small businesses but most were migrant workers from the poorest regions of Tigray who had gone to seek employment as casual labour or as domestic servants in the more favoured cities of their northern neighbour. The estimated 350,000 ethnic Eritreans in Ethiopia tended to be from higher social classes. A sizeable number were senior civil servants or entrepreneurs with substantial business interests. Owing to an unresolved anomaly, the majority of these enjoyed both Ethiopian and Eritrean citizenship.

In the first days of conflict, each leadership sought to reassure the other's nationals that their personal safety was not at risk, the dispute being between the two governments and not between their citizens. As time has gone on, however,

[67] *An Urgent Appeal for Humanitarian Assistance,* Eritrean Relief and Rehabilitation Commission, February 1999.

government spokespeople from each side have claimed – with some justification – that their own people have suffered ill-treatment in the other's territory, in some cases at the hands of officials, in others at the hands of ordinary citizens. Ill-treatment and stories of ill-treatment have grown out of and have fed into negative stereotypes – of the Tigrayans as uncouth peasants and of the ethnic Eritreans as parasites milking dry the Ethiopian economy. Whether or not ill-treatment has been officially instigated, much of the blame for it can be attributed to the vitriolic propaganda which has been disseminated either by the two governments or by their supporters with the governments turning a deaf ear.

The first sign of trouble came very early, on 26 May 1998, when ethnic Eritreans, returning to Ethiopia through the northern crossing point at Rama, reported that Ethiopian immigration officials were removing their Ethiopian ID cards. Nothing similar was reported until 12 June, the day after Eritrea bombed Adigrat, when Ethiopia issued a deportation order on key Eritreans and simultaneously placed Eritrean employees working in 'security-sensitive' positions on enforced leave. Round-ups and detentions continued for three days, and on 15 June a group variously numbered at between 500 and 800 were put on buses and taken northwest to the border at Humera, where they crossed into Eritrea on 17 June.

It seems that deportations were initially provoked by a fear that the Eritreans, whose clandestine networks had helped the EPRDF to secure Addis Ababa in 1991, would use those same networks to undermine a government with which they were now at odds. Most of the first round of detentions and deportations were therefore directed against Eritrean government representatives and against ethnic Eritreans who were known as active EPLF supporters. As the policy continued, however, the net widened and later groups of deportees were almost all Ethiopian citizens who, though of Eritrean origin, had little other connection to Eritrea. Among them were the very old and the very young and, of the latter, many had never been to Eritrea and spoke no Eritrean language. Ethiopia alleges that all of the first deportees and many later ones were 'spies'. Where this is demonstrably not the case – as with the children – the reason for their deportation is given as 'family reunification'. By early 1999, more than 50,000 Eritreans had been deported, sometimes at the rate of more than 1,000 a week.

The method of deportation has followed a standard pattern which has been corroborated by bodies such as Amnesty International.[68] Typically, the police pick up individual family members at night or early in the morning. They are given little or no time to put together their belongings or to prepare for the journey. Their property is confiscated or handed to a relative under a 'power of attorney' that has no legal

[68] Amnesty International, *Ethiopia and Eritrea. Human Rights Issues in a Year of Armed Conflict*, press release, 12 May 1999.

validity. They are held, sometimes for several days, at detention centres and are then transported in buses to the border. Early on, the deportations involved a three- or four-day journey to the northern border but most of the later deportations have been carried out through Assab. At this border point, deportees leave the buses carrying their possessions, and cross 'no man's land' between the front lines on foot before boarding Eritrean buses to the port city. They then travel by boat from Assab to Massawa. In all, it can be several weeks from the time they are picked up until they reach Eritrea.

To the Eritreans' considerable irritation, diplomats and the international media have given very little attention to Ethiopia's treatment of ethnic Eritreans, certainly much less than they have to Eritrean equivocation over the various peace proposals that have been put forward. Individuals and organizations concerned with human rights, notably Mary Robinson, the UN Human Rights Commissioner, Human Rights Watch and Amnesty International, have, however, condemned the deportations. Such condemnations have, in turn, greatly annoyed the Ethiopian authorities who see them as partial, particularly since nothing comparable was said about the more than 120,000 Ethiopians whom the EPLF expelled from Eritrea in 1991.

In any event, Ethiopian legal experts argue that the deportations do not contravene the Geneva Conventions or international laws. Their arguments are partly upheld by other commentators who note that, in time of war, the Conventions do allow states to deport citizens who can be shown to be security risks, though the onus is on governments to prove that the risk exists. International laws also give governments the right to expel, but they ban mass expulsions or expulsions conducted in an arbitrary or discriminatory manner. Judged by these criteria, it appears that Ethiopia's deportations of ethnic Eritreans do fall short of what is required by international human rights legislation. Eritrea, naturally, disputes the legality of any of the deportations. People on both sides of the border view the deportations as a watershed in Ethiopian–Eritrean relations: it is the first time that family and other close social ties have been severed in this way. Most people believe that, at the very least, some form of individual financial restitution will eventually need to be made.

Ethiopians have also been leaving Eritrea over the same period and Ethiopian reports of their number show a certain symmetry with the number of Eritrean deportees, with more than 40,000 recorded as arriving home by the beginning of 1999. The Ethiopian authorities claim that these people are also deportees, thrown out by the Eritrean government, though this is somewhat at odds with their claim that the Eritrean authorities systematically obstruct Ethiopians trying to leave voluntarily. It is, in fact, more common for returnees to claim that they have faced bureaucratic obstruction than that they have been expelled. The Eritrean government denies that any deportations are taking place, claiming rather that Ethiopians are leaving of their own accord, often because they have lost their jobs as a result of economic slow-down.

The Ethiopian government and the private press regularly carry stories alleging atrocities committed against Ethiopians in Eritrea. Many stories describe truly horrific barbarities which, if confirmed, would suggest that at the very least there had been some degree of official collusion. They include allegations of rape by Eritrean soldiers, of acid thrown in women's faces, of men who have died because they were locked in metal containers without food or water in high temperatures for days on end. There are fairly regular reports of Ethiopians attempting to leave who have been paraded in the streets of Eritrea's larger towns, of detentions, beatings, eviction, withholding of wages and robbery. Many of these stories identify the 'Sawa kids', the young National Service conscripts, as the chief culprits. However, no systematic effort has been made by either the Ethiopian government or independent bodies to corroborate these allegations and, off the record, independent observers are sceptical about many of the more lurid stories carried by the Ethiopian media.

In summary, Amnesty International concludes: 'There have been mass expulsions in cruel and inhuman conditions of Eritreans from Ethiopia. The Eritrean security forces ill-treated some Ethiopians but there was no evidence found of a systematic policy in Eritrea of deliberate or widespread ill-treatment of Ethiopians.'[69]

[69] Ibid.

10 THE SEARCH FOR PEACE

On 15 May 1998, just two days after the conflict became public, President Hassan Gouled Aptidon of Djibouti arrived in Addis Ababa offering to mediate to end the hostilities. Two days later US Assistant Secretary of State Susan Rice flew into the Ethiopian capital, with a team of diplomats, on a mediation mission of her own. President Aptidon, never in the best of health and well into his eighties, was an important regional actor, even if the state he led is one of the smallest and poorest in the world. The youthful Ms Rice came on behalf of the world's only superpower. That they should both arrive in the region within days of the hostilities is an indication of just how seriously both the countries of the region and the wider international community took the outbreak of fighting. From the first there has been intensive, ongoing and energetic international diplomatic engagement with the problem.

African countries from Zimbabwe to Egypt, from Kenya to Burkina Faso have actively attempted to stop the war. The United States has been working at the problem from the first and has been supported by Italy, France, Germany and the United Kingdom. The Organization of African Unity, the United Nations and the European Community have put time and effort into resolving the conflict. The Pope has made appeals and offered prayers for peace. Individual negotiators, including Mohammed Sahnoun of the UN and the US special envoy, Anthony Lake, have visited the region repeatedly. Yet the two parties have been remarkably resistant to the combined diplomacy, threats, blandishments and appeals of the outside world. More than a year after the fighting erupted no solution has been found.

At the same time the diplomatic activity has not been entirely without results. Three concrete achievements have been chalked up. First, an outline of a settlement is now on the table. Second, international assistance has been provided to those displaced by the conflict. Third, a cease-fire in the air was successfully negotiated by President Clinton, although this has now collapsed.

A formal proposal for a full cease-fire, with an indication of how the conflict might be resolved, was actually worked out remarkably rapidly by the United States and Rwanda, and presented to both countries on 30 May 1998.[70] This was then

---

[70] Appendix 1.

taken up and worked on intensively by the Organization of African Unity, and was tabled on 7 November.[71] The Ethiopians declared on 11 November 1998 that they had formally accepted the OAU proposals, and on 27 February 1999 the Eritreans followed suit, after receiving answers to a series of detailed questions.[72] In July 1999 a document laying out how the Framework Agreement might be implemented was tabled at the OAU summit in Algiers.[73] This was agreed by both countries. Rather than engage in a blow-by-blow account of the myriad meetings that have taken place over the months, it may be more instructive to consider the obstacles that have prevented more rapid progress towards a solution.

Ethiopia was broadly satisfied with the US–Rwandan proposals, and declared as much, stating that they were 'in line in substance with the position of the Ethiopian Government on the crisis'.[74] The Eritreans, on the other hand, found much to be dissatisfied with. Privately they complained bitterly that the Americans under Susan Rice had attempted to 'bounce' them into accepting the proposals, copies of which were released to the press before Asmara had even had sight of them.[75]

There was also much in the detail that was deeply unsatisfactory from an Eritrean point of view, in particular point two of the plan, which called for an Eritrean withdrawal from Badme and the re-establishment of Ethiopian administration in the area. This would leave the area, which was at the crux of the dispute, firmly in Ethiopian hands. And although point two states plainly that such a withdrawal would be 'without prejudice to the territorial claims of either party', the Eritreans believed that possession was nine-tenths of the law.

This view was probably strengthened by their dispute with Yemen over the Hanish islands in the Red Sea that erupted in December 1995. After some clashes both countries were persuaded to submit their quarrel to the Permanent Court of Arbitration in the Hague. The initial hearings took place in February 1998 and Eritrea knew they were not going well. In its final arbitration the Court awarded the majority of the islands to Yemen, a decision that Eritrea accepted despite considerable misgivings, since it had promised to be bound by the outcome. In essence Eritrea lost the case because it could be shown that such administration as had been exercised over the islands had come from Yemen. As the Tribunal put it, 'on balance … the weight of the evidence supports Yemen's assertions of the exercise of the functions of state authority'.[76] Since Eritrea accepted that the Badme area had been continuously under Ethiopian authority, both before and after independence in 1993, this was

[71] Appendix 2.
[72] Appendix 3.
[73] Appendix 4.
[74] Ethiopian Foreign Ministry statement, 12 August 1998.
[75] *The Economist*, 8 May 1999, p. 77.
[76] Permanent Court of Arbitration, 'The Eritrea–Yemen Arbitration', 9 October 1998, p. 151.

deeply worrying. It is probably for this reason that Asmara has placed such weight on the evidence contained in the Ethiopian treaties with Italy following the battle of Adua in 1896, rather than any more recent events. These concerns are reflected in the close questioning of the OAU on these issues, in particular on those relating to the administration of Badme and the status of colonial treaties.[77]

For precisely the same reasons Ethiopia makes no reference to these treaties in its explanation of the conflict, preferring, instead, to base its claim on the fact that Badme has 'never been under the jurisdiction of an administration whose centre had been Eritrea'.[78]

Indeed, it is remarkable that Ethiopia has consistently refused to state just where it believes its border with Eritrea should lie, or what should determine its location. Most recently Prime Minister Meles Zenawi told the Africa editor of *The Economist* that the map produced in 1997 did not reflect Ethiopia's territorial claims, but he again insisted that he would not say what these claims might be.[79]

Eritrea maintains that since it has now withdrawn from Badme there is no reason why the remaining elements of the OAU proposals cannot be implemented immediately, starting with a formal cease-fire. Ethiopian Prime Minister Meles Zenawi, however, has already told the OAU that his government interprets the phrase in the framework agreement referring to the withdrawal from 'Badme and environs' to mean all occupied territories. The OAU 'took note' of this position but has offered no formal clarification. The contested phrase has certainly been one cause of the continuing stalemate.

This failure of the OAU to provide clarification has been the source of considerable frustration at the UN Security Council. Privately, some Council members have apparently let it be known that they would prefer to take a very literal interpretation, 'Badme and environs' meaning Badme town and the immediate surrounding area. The stance of the Security Council has therefore been to repeat periodically its earlier calls for a cessation of hostilities and the immediate implementation of the OAU proposals. The United States has called for an immediate cease-fire without preconditions, to be followed by a withdrawal by both sides to positions held before the beginning of the conflict.[80]

Meanwhile, in an interview in April broadcast on the Voice of America, Meles Zenawi appeared to soften his tone very slightly.[81] He suggested that a cease-fire agreement might be possible prior to a withdrawal of troops, but only if the Eritreans were willing to provide a formal undertaking to withdraw unilaterally within a given

[77] See Appendix 3, questions 3 and 5.
[78] Ethiopian Foreign Ministry statement, 12 August 1998.
[79] *The Economist*, 8 May 1999, p. 74.
[80] Associated Press, 26 April 1999.
[81] Voice of America, 13 April 1999.

timetable. 'We are not saying they have to withdraw first before there is a cease-fire', the Prime Minister said. 'I mean, they cannot withdraw without a cease-fire. How do you implement that?' Eritrea dismissed this as playing with words.

As noted above, proposals to break this stalemate came before the OAU summit in July. Eritrea immediately accepted, as did Ethiopia a few days later. The United States, whose mediator, Anthony Lake, was at the summit, together with his UN counterpart, Mohammed Sahnoun, welcomed this development. Mr Lake subsequently visited both capitals, in an attempt to turn the proposals into reality and implement the 'Modalities' outlined in Algiers.

11 CONCLUSION

The conflict has not only taken a terrible toll in human life; its costs in economic terms are incalculable, bringing yet more suffering to a region that is one of the poorest on earth. Nor is this confined to the two parties to the fighting. Whatever the outcome of the war, it has already exacerbated existing serious stresses and strains in the region. Both countries are now undertaking 'proxy' operations in neighbouring countries. Sudan, Djibouti, Somaliland, Somalia and Kenya have been, and are being, destabilized by these activities. Eritrea has been active among the Oromos, Somalis and in Djibouti among the Afars; and Ethiopia in Somalia, in Djibouti, and among Afars in Eritrea. The effects of these activities will remain for a long time to come.

The conflict has also raised specific questions of human rights, including the manner of deportations, the treatment of prisoners, the use of land mines. These add to already serious concerns in both states about democracy, accountability, transparency and good governance, nearly always among the first casualties in any conflict. The economic effects have also been profound, affecting in particular the highland peasant population from whom the Tigrayan and even the Eritrean elites draw much of their support and legitimacy. It was they who stood to gain most from a programme of economic integration and the free movement of labour, capital and goods across the region.

Since February 1999 the differences between Addis Ababa and Asmara on how best to resolve the crisis have been tantalizingly small. Both now accept the OAU framework proposals. Both say that they want a negotiated solution. Both declare that they abhor the continuing war, with its loss of life and huge drain on their meagre resources. But a final resolution remains to be found. The only satisfactory explanation for this intransigence can be derived from the ultimate war aims of both sides. It may well be that the leaderships of both Eritrea and Ethiopia now believe that there can be no peace in the region while the other remains in power. President Isaais Afeworki and Prime Minister Meles Zenawi both appear to have concluded that the other must be removed, by fair means or foul, as the price of peace.[82] If that is the case, then the prospects for the Horn of Africa are grim indeed.

[82] 'Fathers and mothers of Ethiopia, you should rise up and oppose the forcible conscription of your sons. The war is an exercise the sole aim of which is to prolong the life of the oppressive regime. We make a friendly call to the Ethiopian people to look for ways in which to rid themselves of the oppressive *woyane* [TPLF] regime' (Voice of the Broad Masses of Eritrea, Asmara, in Oromo, 1600 GMT, 6 May 1999). Documents found on the bodies of dead Ethiopian soldiers are said to indicate that Addis Ababa is plotting to change the government in Asmara. 'We have documents where they are talking of a transitional government, they have regrouped elements from opposition movements. They say that they feel that the only way that the region could be at peace is that there is a change of government in Asmara,' said Eritrean government spokesman, Yemane Gebremeskel (AFP, 11 May 1999).

APPENDIX I

The US–Rwandan plan, presented to both parties on 30–31 May 1998

Press statement by James P. Rubin, US Department of State, 3 June 1998

At the request of both parties, for more than two weeks the Governments of the United States and Rwanda have been engaged in intensive efforts to facilitate a peaceful resolution of the dispute between Eritrea and Ethiopia.

The objective of the joint American–Rwandan facilitation effort has been to promote a peaceful and durable settlement of this dispute and to prevent a war, which would cost many lives and undermine regional stability. Having excellent relations with the Governments of both Eritrea and Ethiopia, the United States and Rwanda have sought to encourage both parties to protect the peace that has taken root in the Horn of Africa since 1991. Throughout our facilitation effort, we urged both parties to exercise restraint.

The facilitation team listened carefully to the detailed positions of both parties and attempted to take full account of their respective perspectives and interests without making any judgement as to where the disputed border lies or what actions may have precipitated the crisis that began with the border skirmish on 6 May.

Based on our consultations, it is clear to the United States and Rwanda that there are many areas of commonality between the two parties and that there exists a practical, principled basis for peaceful resolution of this conflict. Thus, the facilitators presented recommendations to both parties on 30–31 May and asked each party to confirm its acceptance of these recommendations.

The US–Rwandan recommendations are summarized as follows:

(1) Both parties should commit themselves to the following principles: resolving this and any other dispute between them by peaceful means; renouncing force as a means of imposing solutions; agreeing to undertake measures to reduce current tensions; and seeking the final disposition of their common border, on the basis of established colonial treaties and international law applicable to such treaties.

(2) To reduce current tensions, and without prejudice to the territorial claims of either party, a small observer mission should be deployed to Badme; Eritrean forces should redeploy from Badme to positions held before May 6, 1998; the previous civilian administration should return; and there should be an investigation into the events of May 6, 1998.

(3) To achieve lasting resolution of the underlying border dispute, both parties should agree to the swift and binding delimitation and demarcation of the Eritrea–Ethiopian border. Border delimitation should be determined on the basis of established colonial treaties and international law applicable to such treaties, and the delimitation and demarcation process should be completed by a qualified technical team as soon as possible. The demarcated border should be accepted and adhered to by both parties, and, upon completion of demarcation, the legitimate authorities assume jurisdiction over their respective sovereign territories.

(4) Both parties should demilitarize the entire common border as soon as possible.

Finally, the facilitators presented both sides with a detailed implementation plan and recommended that each party convey, in legal and binding manner, its acceptance of the above recommendations and implementation plan to the facilitators.

The United States and Rwanda regret that these recommendations have not yet been accepted by both sides as the basis for a peaceful resolution of this dispute. We are gravely concerned by the resumption of hostilities in recent days, which will render more difficult efforts to achieve a peaceful outcome.

As friends of the Governments of Eritrea and Ethiopia, the United States and Rwanda call on both sides to avoid an escalation of the conflict, to reaffirm their commitment to a peaceful resolution of this dispute, to halt the fighting and to accept without delay the facilitators' recommendations as the basis for a peaceful resolution of this conflict. We remain committed to helping both sides achieve a peaceful settlement and avoid wider conflict through pursuit of further diplomatic efforts.

The Rwandan Government is issuing a statement on this important matter as well.

APPENDIX 2

Organization of African Unity proposal for a framework agreement for a peaceful settlement of the dispute between Eritrea and Ethiopia[83]

[The proposal was presented to the OAU High Level Delegation meeting held in Ouagadougou, Burkina Faso, on 7–8 November 1998 attended by the Presidents of Burkina Faso, Blaise Compaore, Zimbabwe's Robert Mugabe and Djibouti's Hassan Gouled Aptidon and the representative of the UN Secretary General, Mohammed Sahnoun. The proposals were based on the earlier US–Rwandan plan, and was endorsed at the OAU summit held in Ouagadougou on 17–18 December 1998.]

We recommend that:

1. The two Parties commit themselves to an immediate cessation of hostilities;
2. In order to defuse tension and build confidence, the two Parties commit themselves to put an end to any action and any form of expression likely to exacerbate the climate of hostility and tension between them thereby jeopardizing the efforts aimed at finding a peaceful solution to the conflict;
3. In order to create conditions conducive to a comprehensive and lasting settlement of the conflict through delimitation and demarcation of the border, the armed forces presently in Badme Town and its environs should be redeployed to the positions they held before 6 May 1998 as a mark of goodwill and consideration for our continental Organization, it being understood that this redeployment will not prejudge the final status of the area concerned, which will be determined at the end of the delimitation and demarcation of the border and, if need be, through an appropriate mechanism of arbitration;
4. This redeployment be supervised by a Group of Military Observers which will be deployed by the OAU with the support of the United Nations. The Groups of Military Observers will also assist the reinstated Civilian Administration in the maintenance of law and order during the interim period;
5. (a) The redeployment be subsequently extended to all other contested areas along the common border within the framework of demilitarization of the entire common border and as a measure for defusing the tension and facilitating the

[83] *Source:* Organization of African Unity.

65

delimitation and demarcations process. In effect, the demilitarization which will begin with the Mereb Setit segment, will then extend to the Bada area and the border as a whole;

(b) The demilitarization process be supervised by the Group of Military Observers;

6. (a) The two parties commit themselves to make use of the services of experts of the UN Cartographic Unit, in collaboration with the OAU and other experts agreed upon by the two Parties, to carry out the delimitation and demarcation of the border between the two countries within a timetable of six months which could be extended on the recommendation of the cartographic experts;

(b) Once the entire border has been delimited and demarcated, the legitimate authority will immediately exercise full and sovereign jurisdiction over the territory which will have been recognized as belonging to them.

7. In order to determine the origins of the conflict, an investigation to be carried out of the incidents of 6 May 1998 and of any other incident prior to that date which could have contributed to a misunderstanding between the two Parties regarding their common border, including the incidents of July–August 1997.

8. (a) At the humanitarian level, the two Parties commit themselves to put an end to measures directed against the civilian population and refrain from any action which can cause further hardship and suffering to each other's nationals;

(b) the two Parties also commit themselves to addressing the negative socio-economic impact of the crisis on the civilian population, particularly those persons who had been deported;

(c) In order to contribute to the establishment of a climate of confidence, the OAU, in collaboration with the United Nations, deploy a team of Human Rights Monitors in both countries;

9. (a) In order to determine the modalities for the implementation of a Framework Agreement, a Follow-up Committee of the two Parties be established under the auspices of the OAU High-Level Delegation with the active participation and assistance of the United Nations;

(b) The Committee begin its work as soon as the Framework Agreement is signed;

10. The OAU and the UN working closely with the international community, particularly the European Union, endeavour to mobilize resources for the resettlement of displaced persons and the demobilizing of troops currently deployed along the common border of both countries;

11. The Organization of African Unity, in close co-operation with the United Nations, will be the guarantor for the scrupulous implementation of all the provisions of the Framework Agreement, in the shortest possible time.

APPENDIX 3

Issues raised by Eritrea concerning the framework document[84]

1. Regarding Badme and Environs
    (a) On the co-ordinates of Badme and its location relative to the recognized boundary.
    The OAU High-Level Delegation addressed the issue of the Administration of Badme. The issue of the co-ordinates of Badme was not raised. This is a technical matter which could be addressed during the implementation of the Framework Agreement.
    (b) What is meant by environs? Which areas does it include?
    Environs refer to the area surrounding Badme Town.
    (c) According to Ethiopia, 'Badme and environs' means 'all Ethiopian border territories occupied by Eritrea since May 6, 1998'. What is the OAU's view?
    See paragraph 36 in the Report on the efforts of the OAU High-Level Delegation to the Fourth Ordinary Session of the Central Organ, meeting at Heads of State Level, which states: 'the High Level Delegation took note of the position of Prime Minister Meles Zenawi. There was, however, no further discussion on the issue.'
    (d) Has Ethiopia submitted to the OAU the totality of its claims as had been repeatedly requested by Eritrea?
    Ethiopia has indicated that it will submit its claims when the issues of delimitation, demarcation and, if need be, arbitration are addressed.

2. Regarding Re-deployment
    (a) What is the justification for unilateral Eritrean re-deployment from Badme?
    The OAU High Level Delegation came to the conclusion that Badme town and its environs were administered by Ethiopia prior to the events of 6–12 May, 1998. Therefore, the troops to be re-deployed are those that occupied the area between 6–12 May 1998.

---

[84] The OAU reply is given in italics. According to Eritrea, these questions were submitted to the OAU Secretary General during his visit to Asmara on 12 December 1998 and the replies were received on 26 January 1999.
Source: Statement to the UN Security Council, 22 March 1999, by the Eritrean ambassador to the UN; Walta news agency, 13 February 1999.

(b) Why re-deployment to positions before May 6? Where precisely are the positions?

The incidents between 6–12 May are the fundamental issues that brought the dispute to the attention of the OAU and the International Community. The precise location of these positions [is] to be identified by Technical Experts during the implementation states of the Framework Agreement with co-operation of the two parties.

(c) What does 'the re-deployment to be extended within the framework of demilitarization' mean? Whose re-deployment is it?

The re-deployment is of Eritrean troops from Badme Town and its environs. This should be immediately followed by the demilitarisation of the entire border, through the re-deployment of the forces of both parties along the entire border, to positions to be determined subsequently, as part of the implementation process of the Framework Agreement.

3. Regarding Civilian Administration

(a) What is the justification for 'reinstated civilian administration' if the area under consideration is Eritrean with an Eritrean population?

This is based on the conclusions of the OAU High Level Delegation on the Administration of the area concerned prior to 6 May, 1998 and not on the population. This position is without prejudice to the final status of the areas concerned which will be determined after the processes of delimitation, demarcation, and if need be, arbitration, have been concluded.

(b) What is the rationale for setting up an alien administration for a short time when options exist for quick demarcation?

The administration referred to is not a new one; it is the one that was there prior to 6 May, 1998. The High Level Delegation is of the view that this measure will contribute towards defusing tension and paving the way for the implementation of the other aspects of the Framework Agreement.

4. Regarding Investigation

(a) What is the purpose of 'an investigation of the incidents of July–August 1997 and 6 May 1998 and all incidents in between', if it has no bearing on the settlement of the dispute?

The High Level Delegation is of the view that such an investigation has a bearing on a lasting settlement of the dispute. It will provide further clarity on those events, and allow the OAU to appreciate the problem in all its dimensions. In the meantime, the recommendations on re-deployment and demilitarisation are aimed at creating an enabling environment for the processes of delimitation, demarcation and arbitration.

(b) Why are the incidents that occurred on May 6, and that escalated through a series of spiralling clashes until May 12, not seen as one integral act of violation? Moreover, why is May 6, 1998 seen as central? Why not July 1997? *See response in 2 (b).*

5. Regarding Colonial Treaties
    (a) Has the OAU ascertained that both sides recognize and respect the colonial boundary between the two countries as defined by the established colonial treaties?
    This is a fundamental principle of the OAU which all OAU Member States have accepted. This principle is therefore reflected in the proposals submitted by the OAU High Level Delegation to both parties. The OAU takes it that by accepting these proposals and eventually by signing the Framework Agreement which contains this principle, the two Parties would have committed themselves to abiding by this principle.
    (b) If this is the case, can this be affirmed through an agreement between the two Parties?
    This principle is part and parcel of the Framework Agreement.
    (c) What is the meaning of the clause 'international law applicable to the colonial treaties'?
    International laws are laws that govern the relations between States. In this particular case, international law would refer to the specific aspects of the international law relevant to the colonial treaties.
    (d) What is the precise interpretation of the OAU and UN Charters concerning colonial treaties?
    As far as the OAU is concerned, it is to be noted that its Charter refers to the principle of territorial integrity of its Member States. This position was further elaborated on in the well known Resolution AGH/Res. 16 (1) adopted at the OAU Summit in Cairo in July 1964 which provided in its operative paragraphs as follows:

    > *SOLEMNLY REAFFIRMS the strict respect by all Member States of the Organization for the Principles laid down in paragraph 3 of Article III of the Charter of the Organization of African Unity;*
    > *SOLEMNLY DECLARES that all Member States pledge themselves to respect the borders existing on their achievement of national independence.*

6. Regarding Demarcation
    (a) What is the legal basis for demarcation?
    The signing of the Framework Agreement by the two Parties.

(b) What are the modalities, mechanism and time-frame?

The time-frame is 6 months to be extended as provided for in the Framework Agreement (on the recommendation of the cartographic experts).

The modalities and mechanisms to be worked out by the Follow-up Committee in consultation with the Experts.

(c) What are the legal arrangements that will render the outcome binding?

Same response as in 6 (a).

7. The Principle of the Non-Use of Force and Intimidation

    (a) Has the Committee attempted to ascertain which party has used force as a means of imposing a solution?

    This will be determined by the investigations to be carried out as part of the comprehensive settlement plan.

    (b) Has the Committee tried to ascertain which party resorted to force in the July 1997 incident at Adi Murug, the January 1998 incident on the Assab road and the May incidents in Badme?

    The July 1997 and May 1998 incidents will be the subject of the proposed investigation. The January 1998 incident is new to the OAU but could be covered by the investigation as proposed in the Framework Agreement where reference is made to the need to investigate other incidents that may have contributed to the present dispute.

    (c) What is the position of the Committee regarding the resolution of Ethiopia's Parliament on May 13, 1998 declaring war against Eritrea?

    The Committee has refrained from making any judgement on Statements by the Governments and institutions in both countries. It has consistently appealed to both Parties to exercise restraint and refrain from any actions and decisions which could harm the relations between the two sisterly countries and their peoples.

    On the rest of the clarification sought under 7, the Committee considers its role to be one of offering good offices to both Parties and urging them to exercise maximum restraint, as well as to opt for a peaceful settlement of their dispute.

8. Regarding the Principle of a Peaceful Solution to the Disputes

    (a) Which Party has been routinely rejecting a peaceful solution?

    Both Parties have consistently expressed to the OAU High-Level Delegation their commitment to a peaceful settlement of the current dispute.

    (b) Is unconditional cessation of hostilities acceptable to both sides?

    The OAU High-Level Delegation did not address the issue of unconditional cessation of hostilities. It has taken the issues of cessation of hostilities within the context of the Framework Agreement submitted to both sides. In fact, the cessation of hostilities is contained in the first paragraph of the Framework Agreement.

9. Regarding the Violation of Basic Human Rights of Citizens
   (a) Has the Committee taken stock of the basic violations committed and property illegally confiscated?
   See the relevant paragraph in the introductory note handed over to both parties by the Ministerial Committee in Ouagadougou (1–2 August 1998) which stated, inter alia, 'As regards the situation of Eritreans in Ethiopia ... the conditions in which those deportations were carried out, the decision to extend those measures to families of the deported persons and the fate of their properties are a source of deep concern'.
   (b) What will be the role of the OAU in ensuring that these violations are redressed?
   The OAU, with the co-operation of both Parties and with the assistance of the United Nations and other relevant institutions, will help the Parties to address all aspects of the dispute, including the humanitarian problems generated by the dispute.

10. Regarding the Central Organ of the OAU
    (a) What is the mandate of the Central Organ?
    See the 1993 Cairo Declaration of the OAU Summit establishing the Mechanism for Conflict Prevention, Management and Resolution.
    (b) What can we expect from the forthcoming meeting of the Central Organ?
    See the Communiqué adopted by the Central Organ at the end of its deliberations.

APPENDIX 4

Modalities for the Implementation of the OAU Framework Agreement on the Settlement of the Dispute Between Ethiopia and Eritrea[85]

The two Parties reaffirm their commitment to the principle of the non-use of force to settle disputes.

The two Parties reaffirm their acceptance of the Framework Agreement and commit themselves to implement it in good faith.

There shall be a return to positions held prior to 6 May 1998.

On the basis of these principles, the two Parties agree on the following modalities for the implementation of the Framework Agreement:

The Eritrean Government commits itself to redeploy its forces outside the territories they occupied after 6 May 1998.

The Ethiopian Government commits itself to redeploy, thereafter, its forces from positions taken after 6 February 1999 and which were not under Ethiopian administration before 6 May 1998.

The two Parties agree to put an end to all military activities and all forms of expression likely to sustain and exacerbate the climate of hostility and thus compromise the implementation of the Framework Agreement.

The redeployment of troops shall commence immediately after the cessation of hostilities. This redeployment shall not, in any way, prejudice the final status of the territories concerned, it being understood that this status will be determined at the end of the border delimitation and demarcation.

The modalities for the re-establishment of the civilian Administration and population in the concerned territories shall be worked out after the cessation of hostilities.

The two Parties accept the deployment of Military Observers by the OAU in cooperation with the United Nations. The Group of Military Observers will supervise the redeployment of troops as stipulated in the present modalities and carry out all other

[85] This was proposed at the 35th OAU summit in Algeria in July 1999.
Source: Embassy of Eritrea, Washington, DC, 14 July 1999.

72

duties that are entrusted to it, in conformity with the relevant provisions of the Framework Agreement.

The two Parties commit themselves to sign a formal Ceasefire Agreement which provides the detailed modalities for the implementation of the Framework Agreement.

APPENDIX 5

Eritrean opposition groups making up the Alliance of Eritrean National Forces (AENF)

The Eritrean Liberation Front (Abdullah Idris).

The ELF – Revolutionary Council.

The ELF National Congress.

Two factions of the Eritrean Islamic Jihad (now called the Eritrean People's Congress and the Eritrean Islamic Salvation Movement).

Three small Marxist groups, previously based in Ethiopia (the Popular Democratic Front for the Liberation of Eritrea, the Eritrean Revolutionary Democratic Front – itself formerly the Democratic Movement for the Liberation of Eritrea – and the ELF – Central Command).

Two Kunama groups (the Eritrean Kunama Democratic Movement and the Eritrean Democratic Resistance Movement [Gash-Setit]).

The Khartoum-based Eritrean Initiative Group and an individual, Ali Muhammed Sayyid Berhatu, formerly chairman of the ELF – United Organization, and more recently adviser to the Afar Sultan Alimirreh of Assieta.

APPENDIX 6

Somali groups receiving Ethiopian support

Ethiopia has provided support including arms and finances to the Somali National Front (Marehan clan) in Gedo region; the RRA (Rahenwene) in Bay and Bakool regions; the United Somali Congress–Peace Movement (Hawadle/Hawiye) in Belet Weyne in central Somalia; Hussein Haji Bod's faction of the United Somali Congress (Abgal/Hawiye); the Somali Salvation Democratic Front (Majerteen) of Colonel Abdullai Yusuf, now the government of Puntland in northeastern Somalia; and the Somali Popular Movement (Majerteen/Harti) of General Mohammed Siyad Hersi 'Morgan' in Kismayo.

Somali groups receiving Eritrean support

Somali National Alliance of Hussein 'Aydeed' (Hawiye clan); Somali Salvation Alliance of Ali Mahdi (Hawiye). Also allied to Hussein 'Aydeed' are factions of the Somali Popular Movement under Colonel Ahmed Jess and the Somali National Front under General Omar Haji Mohamed.